*Spirit-Filled*

# GUIDE

*by*
*Ralph M. Riggs*

**GOSPEL PUBLISHING HOUSE**
Springfield, Missouri 65802

**02-0588**

[ PRINTED
IN U·S·A ]

# Preface

In the year 1931, the book *A Successful Pastor* was published. The intervening years have provided opportunity for additional pastoral experience and administrative work among pastors and churches Ministry at Ministers' Institutes and Seminars has necessitated consideration of many angles of pastoral and evangelistic work, and open forums and general discussion periods have brought out further questions and problems which required answer.

As a means of doing the most good to the most pastors in the most accessible and ready way, the results of this additional experience are now given my fellow ministers in THE SPIRIT-FILLED PASTOR'S GUIDE.

—R. M. R.

# Contents

## E. *THE MINISTER AND HIS MESSAGE*

## F. *THE MINISTER AMONG HIS PEOPLE*

## G. *GENERAL ADMONITION AND EXAMPLE*

CHAPTER 1

# The Call to Preach

THE very first question in all things concerning the minister is whether or not he is actually called of God to preach the gospel. If he is not, he would do well to close this book and forget the matter. It is not the purpose of this book to enable one to acquire a knowledge of the art of pastoring a church if one has not first actually and personally been "sent" into God's harvest. Matt. 9:38.

There is a sense in which all Christians are called to preach or to proclaim the gospel. In 1 Cor. 12:13 we are reminded that by one Spirit are we all baptized into one body and have all been made to drink into one Spirit. We know very well that the life and nature of the Lord Jesus Christ, our Divine Head, is one of love for lost souls and of an intense spirit of evangelism. Luke 19:10. If our Master and Head pours out His life for the lost and seeks continuously to save them, is it to be wondered at that the body which partakes of the life and nature of the Head should likewise be intent upon the salvation of the lost? Anything less would prove, in equal measure, a lack of vital relationship between the body and the Head. The same figure is used in Rom. 12:4, 5 declaring that we are one body in Christ and, being in Christ, are in His very life and nature. The figure of the vine and its branches is used in John 15:1-8. He being the vine and we the branches, we abide in Him and draw from Him the very life that sustains us; and with that life we bear fruit on behalf of the vine. We are merely channels through which the life of the vine flows for the production of the fruit.

A distinction between the ministry and the laity which holds that the evangelistic love of Christ is reserved for the ministry and confined to them is distinctly contrary to the teaching of the Word and the desire of Christ. In His message to the churches at Ephesus and Pergamos, the Lord declared plainly that He hated the doctrine and the deeds of the Nicolaitanes. Rev. 2:6, 15. This, it is thought, was the name of an early sect of Christians who believed that the laity should be ruled over and that the ministers should monopolize Christian ministry. The Lord had declared plainly, in Matt. 23:8, "All ye are brethren." He surely means that brotherhood, comradeship, and Holy Ghost democracy should prevail among the members of His body. It is very definitely therefore the will of God that the great evangelistic passion of our Divine Head shall not be confined to the ministry but shall find expression through every member of His church.

As the Lord sent His first disciples out to preach the gospel to all the world, He gave them instructions concerning their converts. The apostles were told clearly to go and teach all nations (Matt. 28:19), to go into all the world and preach the gospel to every creature (Mark 16:15, 16), and also that repentance and remission of sins should be preached in His name among all nations beginning at Jerusalem (Luke 24:47). There is therefore no doubt that the apostles were commissioned to carry the gospel of salvation to all nations and to every creature. And Matt. 28:20 declares plainly that when they made converts and baptized them in water in the name of the Father, and of the Son, and of the Holy Ghost, they were to teach these converts to observe all things whatsoever He had commanded them. The command then to evangelize the world which came to the first disciples from the lips of Jesus was to be transferred and passed on by them to every convert which they would make. This means that all of us as their remote converts are likewise instructed to preach the gospel unto all nations and to every creature. As a matter of fact, the Lord Himself actually remembered us in His great high-priestly prayer saying, "Neither pray I for these alone, but for them also which shall believe on Me through their word." John 17:20.

It is also true that all believers have been empowered by the Lord's own authority to do the same works that He did and even to do greater. John

[ 3 ]

14:12. Signs which Christian workers were to have follow their ministry were in reality said to follow "them that believe." Mark 16:17. Note that it does not say, "These signs shall follow the apostles or preachers," but the promise is to those who heard —those creatures in all the world who heard the gospel and who believed and were saved. To these converts near and remote there was given this dynamic promise, "These signs shall follow them that believe."

The baptism of the Holy Spirit was said specifically to be a divine anointing for the preaching of the gospel to the ends of the earth. "But ye shall receive power, after that the Holy Ghost is come upon you: and ye shall be witnesses unto Me both in Jerusalem, and in all Judea, and in Samaria, and unto the uttermost part of the earth." Acts 1:8. Peter, in Acts 2:39, tells us plainly that the baptism of the Holy Spirit was not only for the Jews of his audience on the day of Pentecost but "to all that are afar off, even as many as the Lord our God shall call." Thus all who are called of God from sin unto salvation are entitled to receive the baptism of the Holy Spirit which is the enduement with power to witness concerning the gospel. One hundred and twenty, including preachers and laymen, received this baptism on the day of Pentecost. Thousands more continued steadfastly in the apostles' doctrine and fellowship. To those and to all who receive this glorious baptism of the Holy Spirit there comes this clear instruction that all such are to be witnesses of this glorious gospel.

That every Christian is empowered for Christian service and instructed to work for God is further demonstrated and proved by the fact that when all the disciples, except the apostles, were scattered abroad in the persecution that arose at the time of Stephen's martyrdom, they that were scattered abroad went everywhere preaching the Word. Acts 8:1, 4. It was not the apostles that preached the Word in this case but it was all others than the apostles (namely, the regular members of the apostolic church) who went out and proclaimed the way of salvation. These who were scattered abroad travelled as far as to Antioch, and preached the Word. The great missionary church at Antioch was established by lay-preachers. "Then tidings of these things came unto the ears of the church which was in Jerusalem: and they sent forth Barnabas that he should go as far as Antioch." Acts 11:19-22.

This plan of every-member evangelism inaugurated by our Lord and practiced faithfully by the early church resulted in the proclamation of the gospel to every creature of that generation. "Which is come unto you, as it is in all the world; and bringeth forth fruit, as it doth also in you, since the day ye heard of it, and knew the grace of God in truth." "If ye continue in the faith grounded and settled, and be not moved away from the hope of the gospel, which ye have heard, and which was preached to every creature which is under heaven; whereof I Paul am made a minister." Col. 1:6, 23. Thus it has already been demonstrated that, without the aid of the mechanical inventions and conveniences of a modern day, the message can be taken into all the world so that a whole generation of men may hear the gospel through the personal witnessing of the regular members of the Christian church. "But I say, Have they not heard? Yes verily, their sound went into all the earth, and their words unto the ends of the world." Rom. 10:18. Of course, they did not all obey the gospel, but it went out nevertheless "into all the earth, and their words unto the ends of the world." Here is a challenge and a condemnation to the Christians of each generation who do not have the vision, or the faith, or the consecration to obey their Lord and follow the example of their apostolic forebears. Here also is a demonstration of the workableness and effectiveness of having every member of the church busily engaged in witnessing for Christ and spreading the gospel wherever he can. If this generation of Christian people—preachers and laymen— were as filled with the Spirit as the first generation was, then this generation of ours, though it be two billion strong throughout the world, would have the gospel preached unto them.

Without contradicting or disturbing the premise laid down in the previous paragraphs, we can now make another statement which may appear at first to be contrary to that just made. We have stated before that there is a sense in which all church members are called to preach the gospel. We now state that there is also a specific call to preach. Certain individuals have been chosen of the Lord to serve in definite and outstanding ways as propagators of the faith. Before proving this statement by a citation of various Scriptures let us see if we cannot understand the reason and necessity for it and wherein there is harmony and not contradiction in the facts that all are called and also that certain ones are especially called.

A large firm places a sign in the window that help is wanted. In response to this, say one hundred people apply at the office to seek employment in this firm. They are employed and told to report to work the following morning. Upon their arrival in working clothes they present themselves to the foreman to be told just where to work and what to do. They had all been "called" the previous day, but now each must be particularly and especially assigned to his individual task. When a gang of men is hired to erect a building, each must be assigned his specific job by the contractor and his foremen. Different types of workmen are needed, from the architect and his draughtsmen to the contractor, the masons, the carpenters, the plumbers, the electricians, the plasterers, and the common laborers. A wide range of work is required to complete the whole job. All phases of construction work must be harmonized and integrated so that there is no overlapping and no great parts of the job left undone.

The Lord Jesus Christ is indeed "the Lord of the harvest." Matt. 9:38. He is the householder who goes out in the morning to hire laborers for his vineyard. Matt. 20:1. He has the task of evangelizing the world laid out before Him. He needs a great host of workers to perform this task. A wide variety of ministry is needed in order to accomplish this end. His is the over-all intelligence and planning for the efficient and sure completion of this great work. He needs front-line missionaries and evangelists. He needs those devoted to a life of prayer. He must have others to be stewards of the money needed to supply these front-line workers. He needs stayers-at-home as well as go-ers abroad. He needs Sunday School teachers, deacons, ushers, members of adult Sunday School classes, young people's leaders, and members of young people's organizations. Each Christian has his own work to which the Lord of the harvest will assign him. It is the privilege and duty of each member of the family of God, each worker in the Lord's vineyard, to apply directly and personally to Him who is his Master, and receive from Him a specific assignment to the task the Lord has ordained for him to perform. Some He will call to a full-time, out-and-out ministry. But He calls each one to serve in some capacity as a furtherer of the gospel cause. Herein is it true that, although all are called, yet some have specific assignments to full-time ministry and are therefore in a special sense "called to preach."

"And how shall they preach except they be sent?" Rom. 10:15. "For as we have many members in one body, and all members have not the same office: so we, being many, are one body in Christ, and every one members one of another. Having then gifts differing according to the grace that is given to us, whether prophecy, let us prophesy according to the proportion of faith; or ministry, let us wait on our ministering; or he that teacheth, on teaching; or he that exhorteth, on exhortation; he that giveth, let him do it with simplicity; he that ruleth, with diligence; he that showeth mercy, with cheerfulness." Rom. 12:4-8. "Wherefore He saith, When He ascended up on high, He led captivity captive, and gave gifts unto men. . . . And He gave some, apostles; and some, prophets; and some, evangelists; and some, pastors and teachers." Eph. 4:8, 11. The third chapter of First Timothy begins with a description of elders or bishops, and the eighth verse introduces the deacons and their description. Thus in this one chapter two levels or kinds of ministry are indicated. From 1 Cor. 12:11, 18 we learn that the Lord has placed the members in the body as it hath pleased Him.

An interesting revelation of the purpose and plan of God is given us in the first six verses of Exodus 31. Bezaleel and Aholiab were called by name and filled with the Spirit of God to do all manner of workmanship. Their service was that of skilled mechanics and workers in gold, silver and brass and in the cutting of stones. Here are men specifically called and even filled with the Holy Spirit with the end in view that they should be skilled manual laborers. Their secular work was ordained of God. This clearly reveals that God calls some to secular work and equips them for it. So we can expect Him to call many of His own body today to perform secular service.

The early disciples were called away from secular employment as recorded in John 1:35-51 and Matt. 4:19. Young David in 1 Samuel 16:12 was anointed with oil that he should later become king over Israel. Very specifically, likewise, the apostle Paul was called and chosen to bear Christ's name before Gentiles and kings and the children of Israel. Acts 9:15. Thus we have Scriptural precedent for divine calls into full-time ministry. There can be no doubt that God works according to this pattern today. Let those who consider giving their lives to full-time Christian service make sure that they have specific instructions from the Lord of the harvest to this end.

A false call or a running without being sent is indeed a most serious thing. "Thus saith the Lord God; woe unto the foolish prophets, that follow their own spirit, and have seen nothing! They have seen vanity and lying divination, saying, The Lord saith: and the Lord hath not sent them: and they have made others to hope that they would confirm the word." Ezekiel 13:36. Ahimaaz was thrilled by the excitement of the moment and by the example of Cushi, the appointed messenger. He pleaded with Joab for permission to run, and Joab said, "Wherefore wilt thou run, my son, seeing that thou hast no tidings ready?" Upon his further pleading, Joab allowed him to run and with great zeal he outran Cushi. Now he was a good man and very zealous (2 Sam. 18:27) but he had no real message, and the king commanded him to turn aside and stand still. How futile and how embarrassing!

But when the Lord says that He is against these prophets whom He has not sent and who have seen nothing, the situation becomes more serious. Deut. 18:20 declares, "The prophet which shall presume to speak a word in My name, which I have not commanded him to speak . . . even that prophet shall die." It would be better to spend one's life in secular employment doing that which is harmless, even though spiritually useless, than to dabble in this spiritual realm where things are so sacred and holy. Nadab and Abihu brought strange fire into the tabernacle of old; and there went out a fire from the Lord and devoured them, and they died before the Lord. Lev. 10:1, 2. Their father and brothers were not even allowed to mourn their death, for this would seem to be taking their side against the God who had judged them. Better play with forked lightning than trifle with these holy, divine things!

General observation today inclines one to think that there are those who have chosen the ministry as a profession in order to gain social prestige and have opportunity for the display of forensic abilities and social and moral leadership. An opportunity for extensive reading, a comparatively easy life, and professional status in the community, all constitute an allurement to some men today. They have taken away the key of knowledge; they stand in the door of the kindgom of heaven and enter not in, and them that would enter they hinder. Luke 11:52. Blind leaders of the blind, without the knowledge of the way of eternal life and the things of the kingdom, they dare to hold the position of leaders and feeders of the souls of men. Without spirtual life or knowledge, they are unable to convey such to those who hear them. How great must be their condemnation by the people whom they have deceived as well as by the Lord, the Judge of all, at that day!

But some will ask, how can one be called? How can one know that he is called of God into Christian service? How can one avoid the mistake of Ahimaaz and the fatal crime of Nadab and Abihu? How can one make sure that he does not stand, as the Pharisees of old, in the door of the kingdom, not entering himself and blocking the path of others? This is indeed a fair question and one that must have a frank answer.

A call to preach is a spiritual conception. "But the natural man receiveth not the things of the Spirit of God: for they are foolishness unto him: neither can he know them, because they are spiritually discerned." 1 Cor. 2:14. It is one of "the things of the Spirit of God" which the natural man cannot understand but which are nevertheless very real and clear to the regenerate man. The Lord declared in John 10:27, "My sheep hear My voice." This voice is inaudible to the natural ear but is very clear and distinct to the heart of one who is born again. Elijah heard it, and it was called "the still small voice." 1 Kings 19:12. Isaiah said, "Thine ears shall hear a word behind thee, saying, This is the way, walk ye in it." Isa. 30:21. There will be a definite whispering in the deepest soul that the child of God will be conscious of, and it will be his clarion call into the Lord's service.

It will always be true in a call of God that the Lord Himself shall have taken the initiative. "Ye have not chosen Me, but I have chosen you, and ordained you, that ye should go and bring forth fruit, and that your fruit should remain: that whatsoever ye shall ask of the Father in My name, He may give it you." John 15:16. We may not be conscious of this, and may think at first that it was our volunteering for Christian service that started our career in this direction, but the prompting was the Lord's in the first place. It is so much better if we understand this clearly. As it is of His initiative, then His is the responsibility for the whole undertaking. As He sees the end from the beginning, and knows our possibilities and handicaps, and calls us nevertheless into Christian service, we may rest assured that He has figured it all out and knows that He can use us in His harvest field.

The Lord's approach to one, and the manner and method which He chooses in inducting one into His service, may and very likely will be very different to that which He will use in the case of another. Elisha was plowing in the field when Elijah passed by and cast his mantle upon him. 1 Kings 19:19. Samuel came to anoint David and called him from the shepherd's field for the simple ceremony. Amos was no prophet, neither a prophet's son; he was a herdsman and a gatherer of sycamore fruit; and the Lord took him as he followed the flock and said unto him, "Go prophesy unto My people Israel." Amos 7:14, 15. Paul received a heavenly vision but Timothy was chosen by an older preacher to travel with him in gospel work. Acts 26:19; 16:1-3. Let us not therefore seek to receive our call according to patterns used before. Each man is a distinct creation of God and has a right to be called by the Lord in a way which is distinctively his. Let us be satisfied to be our own selves, and let the Lord call us in that way which will fit our natures and which we can understand.

After the original conviction that we are called of God there will come a definite leading step by step as we follow the great Chief Shepherd. We hear His voice and follow Him. John 10:27. "The steps of a good man are ordered by the Lord." Psalm 37:23. "The meek will He guide in judgment: and the meek will He teach His way." Psalm 25:9. It is not declared in what specific way the Holy Ghost spoke in Acts 13:2, but the Bible does say that the Holy Ghost said, "Separate Me Barnabas and Saul for the work whereunto I have called them." When they were on their missionary journey the Holy Spirit checked them to the left and to the right but allowed them free rein straight ahead. Acts 16:6-10. His leading will be as clear and definite as His original call.

A call into the ministry can be analyzed in the following way. Before the call comes it will be true in most cases that there will be a certain natural fitness for the work to which the Lord has called us. A voice that is not difficult to understand, and an appearance that is not objectionable, and an average amount of ability to think and to express oneself, will be good material for the Lord to use.

As the first step, the Lord will breathe upon us of His Spirit and we will become conscious of an interest in and inclination toward His service. It will not be long, however, until this desire on our part will be overshadowed by the sense of our own unworthiness. The desire will still be there but a sense of our own inability will outweigh the inclination which we had felt. This will lead us to a spreading of the whole matter before the Lord and a waiting before Him for the solution. Before long the answer will come. "Not that we are sufficient of ourselves to think anything as of ourselves; but our sufficiency is of God." 2 Cor. 3:5. Like the apostle Paul, we will begin to feel and to say, "I can do all things through Christ which strengtheneth me." Phil. 4:13. Our confidence in God not only will take the place of any self-confidence which we may have had but also will fill up the great cavity of the sense of our unworthiness.

At this time also there will dawn upon us a high estimate of the office to which it seems we are destined. We will realize that this is the most important ministry and life which it is possible for a human to have. Other things are earthly, this is heavenly. Other things are human, this is divine. Other things are for time, this is for eternity. Other things are for the world, the flesh and the devil, but this and this alone is for God.

As the call is clear and His leadings are definite, there will be outcroppings and embryonic expressions of the gift and ministry that will later find their maturity. Our fellow ministers and saints in the family of God will become conscious of the call of God which is resting upon us. There will be a confirmation of our call in numerous ways and a general approval of our desire to serve the Lord as His minister. The ordination which the Lord Himself has given us in the first place will later be confirmed by the ordination of the church and its appointed leaders. This is God's plan for the development of His workers. He has condescended to be yoked together in partnership with His church, and workers in the vineyard receive this double ordination. Finally, the burden will be too great and the pressure too strong for successful resistance. "Woe is me if I preach not the gospel," said Paul. All things are turned to ashes. There is no joy, no peace, no satisfaction in any other occupation or service. With this divine compelling, we are thrust forth into His great harvest field and go forth with the certain conviction that He goes before.

# CHAPTER 2

## Preparation for the Ministry

**P**REPARATION for the ministry can be considered in two phases: experience and education. Inasmuch as we consider experience the greater in importance, we will speak of it first. In considering the general realm of experience which the minister must have in preparation for his work, we think of those crises in one's life which are outstanding and climactic. We also think about the day-by-day experiences of a mature Christian which qualify him to advise others who are passing through similar experiences.

The initial crisis experience that a Christian worker must have is, of course, the new birth. Jesus said: "Verily, verily, I say unto thee, Except a man be born again, he cannot see the kingdom of God." John 3:3. The natural man will never be able to understand the things of the Spirit of God; hence it will be absolutely necessary for one to be given the mind of Christ, a spiritual comprehension. "But the natural man receiveth not the things of the Spirit of

God: for they are foolishness unto him; neither can he know them, because they are spiritually discerned. But he that is spiritual judgeth all things, yet he himself is judged of no man. For who hath known the mind of the Lord, that he may instruct Him? But we have the mind of Christ." 1 Cor. 2:14-16. As a matter of fact, the Lord is angry at the individual who would presume to speak the word of God when he himself is disobedient to those words. "But unto the wicked God saith, What hast thou to do to declare My statutes, or that thou shouldest take My covenant in thy mouth? Seeing thou hatest instruction, and castest My words behind thee." Psalm 50: 16, 17.

Subsequent to the experience of the new birth, there is for every Christian a definite baptism in the Holy Spirit. On the day of Pentecost Peter said, "Repent and be baptized every one of you in the name of Jesus Christ for the remission of sins, and ye shall receive the gift of the Holy Ghost. For the promise is unto you, and to your children, and to all that are afar off, even as many as the Lord our God shall call." Acts 2:38, 39. This is a definite statement to the effect that after repentance and water baptism there is the receiving of the Holy Spirit; and also that this gift of the Holy Ghost is for all whom the Lord our God shall call. The apostles at Jerusalem were not content that the converts at Samaria should abide long without the baptism of the Holy Spirit, but sent unto them Peter and John that they might bring to them this additional glorious

experience. Acts 8:14-17. Paul was addressed by
Ananias as "Brother Saul" before he was filled with
the Holy Ghost. Acts 9:17. Of the disciples at
Ephesus Paul inquired, "Have ye received the Holy
Ghost since (or when) ye believed?" Acts 19:2.
The question would have been pointless and unnecessary if it had been impossible to believe without receiving the baptism in the Holy Ghost. To the
regular church members at Ephesus Paul sent the
command, "Be filled with the Spirit." Eph. 5:18.
Thus it certainly is very clear that the Lord definitely
intended that every Christian should be baptized in
the Holy Spirit in addition to his initial Christian
experience of regeneration.

Now if it is established that there is a baptism of
the Holy Spirit subsequent to conversion and that it
was the normal practice of the early Christians to receive this experience in addition to their conversion,
how can it possibly be proper for one to assume the
position of a leader, teacher and example for the
saints (which, of course, a minister is) unless he himself has first received the Baptism of the Holy Ghost?
Upon the apostles rested the responsibility of preaching repentance and the remission of sins in Christ's
name among all nations. Yet they were told not to
take one step in the execution of this divine, God-
given commission until they were first endued with
the equipment needed; namely, the Baptism of the
Holy Spirit. Luke 24:47-49. This instruction was
repeated by our Lord as recorded in Acts 1:4-8. The
last verse of this passage calls particular attention to

the fact that it was the coming of the Holy Ghost in full baptismal measure which was to give them the power they needed to be witnesses for Him. And how can it be denied that Christians and especially Christian workers today, upon whom rests the same responsibility, need the same power from on high to preach the same gospel to the same unbelieving human heart deceived and held captive by the same Satan? Our conclusion therefore is that no one should be satisfied to preach the gospel of the Lord Jesus Christ without having received the Baptism in the Holy Spirit. This we would consider an absolute essential in the way of preparation for gospel ministry.

It must not be claimed by any means that the Baptism of the Holy Spirit, however wonderful and necessary it is in the way of personal experience and equipment for personal witness, is the hall mark of spiritual perfection. When Peter and John were surrounded by the wondering multitude after the healing of the lame man at the Gate Beautiful, Peter protested that it was not by their own power or HOLINESS that they had made that man to walk. Acts 3:12. The Baptism of the Holy Spirit is the clothing upon with power from on high with which effectually to tell the gospel of the Lord Jesus Christ. But transformation of character and entering into the deeper experiences of the Christ-life should follow in the life of every Christian who is baptized in the Holy Spirit. These day-by-day experiences of walking with God

[ 21 ]

and learning the lessons of the Christian life are also necessary as equipment for effective Christian ministry.

The Christian teacher himself must first learn the things which he is to teach. It will be his prerogative not only to teach doctrine and the general outline of Christian faith but also the actual experiences through which Christians pass in every-day life. The enemy certainly is not just theoretical; he is real and intensely active. He brings against each Christain every conceivable line of attack. It is the pastor's business to take his people by the hand and lead them through bewildering and confusing experiences. While the enemy seeks to defeat and down them, it is the pastor's job to lift them up and establish them in the faith. He is quite unqualified for such ministry unless he himself has gone through similar experiences. One has to go through the mill himself in order to be made bread for others. Walking by faith, for instance, is something that no one can possibly understand unless he himself has learned so to walk. The discovery of Christ as the "form of the Fourth" who is with us in our burning fiery furnace will give us positiveness and joy as we explain to others who are passing through their fiery trial that ever near them too there will be found the presence of the Son of God.

These personal experiences through which prospective pastors must pass may also involve some consecrations that wring their very souls. No one is in a position to serve God effectively who withholds ought from Him. We may serve Him fairly well for a while with unsurrendered areas still within our lives, but the time will come when the Lord will lay His finger upon anything that stands between Him and us. He is a jealous God and His glory and the affections due unto Him will He not allow to be placed upon another. "He that loveth father or mother more than Me is not worthy of Me: and he that loveth son or daughter more than Me is not worthy of Me." Matt. 10:37. "If any man come to Me and hate not his father, and mother, and wife, and children, and brethren and sisters, yea, and his own life also, he cannot be My disciple. And whosoever doth not bear his cross, and come after Me, cannot be My disciple. . . . So likewise, whosoever he be of you that forsaketh not all that he hath, he cannot be My disciple." Luke 14:26, 27, 33.

The Lord Jesus Christ in living reality is our personal teacher and guide and sovereign. He lays definitely upon our souls requirements which must be met in order to follow Him further. Many disciples reach certain points at which they turn aside and follow Him no more. "From that time many of His disciples went back, and walked no more with Him." John 6:60. Those who fall by the wayside are disqualified from being leaders of men and teachers of souls. Paul suffered tremendous persecution and tribulation. He remarked, however, in 2 Cor. 1:4,

5, that these afflictions of Christ in his own life had brought a revelation of the consolation also of Christ. This double experience of suffering and consolation equipped him, he said, to "comfort them which are in any tribulation by the comfort wherewith we ourselves are comforted of God." This experience of the apostle Paul placed him in the position necessary to minister effectively to other Christians who were coming along the same spiritual pathway.

Abraham was called upon to sacrifice his own and dearest, the one in whom were involved the promises of God. It was by his response to this call and his unhesitating willingness to give God his all that God demonstrated that here was a man who was worthy of being called His friend and whom He could make the father of the faithful. We serve the same Jehovah. We may expect Him to make similar demands of us. He would make us, too, His friends. He would make us, also, fathers of the faithful. God may call upon us, too, to surrender the legitimate, good things of life—things which others are allowed to keep and enjoy. Experiences such as these qualify us for Christian ministry. Failure to measure up and obey the call of God will limit us in continued effective ministry in His kingdom.

When God would make a Moses and have him prepared for a spiritual and administrative leadership of His nation of Israel, He not only chose a man who was the most highly trained of all the men of Egypt but He took particular care that this prospective servant should have a long period of spiritual waiting before God and going down in humility as additional preparation for the work to which he was called. We are told in Acts 7:22 that "Moses was learned in all the wisdom of the Egyptians, and was mighty in words and in deeds." Josephus gives us the additional information that Moses was the commander in chief of the armies of Egypt. This is certainly to be expected, for was he not the heir-apparent? He received not only all of the educational and ordinary advantages in the way of accomplishments and skills which were available to the most favored young men of Egypt, but he was given a training which was above all others; for he alone was being prepared to assume the throne at the death of his foster grandfather.

Would not this higher and exceptional training be considered sufficient preparation for the leadership of the nation of Israel? Would not he who was naturally equipped and qualified to lead and rule the many millions of the most civilized nation of the earth at that time surely be sufficiently equipped to lead a much smaller nation of slaves such as the Israelites were? We might answer "Yes," but God answers "No." There is something that one cannot learn in books, on battlefield or athletic grounds, in laboratories, libraries, or lecture halls. There is a fire into which one's soul must be placed in order to receive that purifying and hardening which is necessary for spiritual leadership. Moses saw Him who was invisible, and having respect unto the recompense of the reward he esteemed the reproach of Christ greater riches than the treasures in Egypt. He denied himself the pleasures of sin for a season and chose rather to suffer affliction with the people of God. He refused to be called the son of Pharoah's daughter and by faith he forsook Egypt, not fearing the wrath of the king. Heb. 11:24-27.

In the solitude of the back side of the desert the vision of God's greatness and his own littleness grew and grew. He endured as seeing Him who is invisible, and he diminished in his own estimation. For his own personal satisfaction, for the enjoyment of the realities of life, he was abundantly content to carry the shepherd's crook and quietly look after the sheep. When God at last considered that these forty long years of personal maturing had produced the proper degree of fruition in Moses, He appeared to him in the burning bush. At the announcement that he, Moses, was to lead his own people from the land of Egypt, Moses insisted that he was not eloquent, but slow of speech and of a slow tongue. Ex. 4:10. He had in reality (according to the standards of Egypt) been mighty in words (Acts 7:22), but now he persisted that this was as nothing and that, in reality, he was slow of speech. How great the transformation and descent in self-estimation! This long period of personal testing God considered very valuable in the preparation of His servant.

The apostle Paul was not the product of an accident. He was the product of deliberate preparation on the part of Him whom he served. His natural preparation as a member of the Sanhedrin, highly educated as such members had to be, was by no means sufficient for the ministry to which he was called. His marvelous conversion on the road to Damascus and his Baptism in the Holy Spirit at Damascus likewise were not sufficient. Sitting at the feet of the apostles would not complete his education and provide the adjustment needed for Christian work. There had to be a personal contact with God, and the deliberate and long period of waiting in His presence. To Arabia, another desert, and then back to Damascus for a period of three years; then a brief contact with the apostles and the church at Jerusalem, and off again to Tarsus, his own home town, further to wait upon God and to mature in his own personal experience. This was a most vital part of the preparation of the apostle Paul for the ministry to which he was called. He could have been urged by the enemy to hasten off with his immature knowledge of the way and rush immediately into missionary endeavor, but he was not to be stampeded. He followed his "star." The God who ripens fragile gourds in a few weeks and oak trees over long years of seasoning, chose to prepare this mighty oak of Christian power over a long period of careful growth and development. Even after Barnabas came for him and took him back to the church at Antioch, he continued there in a subordinate capacity until the Holy Ghost called for his separation to the missionary ministry. Paul lingered long at the feet of his Master in humble teachableness until he received the full-orbed revelation of the gospel of grace. Here he acquired the personal character with which to endure the persecutions that were to follow and the power to perform the miracles which later were wrought through his life. He is a pattern to us who follow and echo his gospel and experience.

The word "experience" has another definition. When an individual applies for a position, say as a welder or stenographer, he is usually asked by his prospective employer, "How much experience have you had?" This means how many years or months he has served in actual work in this capacity. By doing the thing himself in the shop or office, he has acquired a certain proficiency which could not be secured as he studied or merely observed others working. There is truly no substitute for actual experience or long practice in doing things. With this definition also of the word experience in mind it can be stated again that the pastor must have experience in order to be qualified for effective ministry.

Joshua was the leader of the children of Israel, succeeding Moses. He led them triumphantly across the Jordan and from victory to victory in the land of Canaan. He was a man who knew God and was instrumental in the hands of God in the performance of mighty miracles (the fall of Jericho, commanding the sun and moon to stand still), as well as in the military conquest of mighty nations, having only an army of former slaves at his command. What was the preparation which the man Joshua received for this spiritual as well as natural leadership? He was a "minister" to Moses for the forty years of the wilderness wandering. Ex. 24:13. "Minister" in this case does not mean pastor, nor has it any professional connotation; frankly, it means that he was the personal servant of Moses for those years. By his intimacy and personal contact with Moses he was allowed certain opportunities to observe the character of this great leader and also to see how God dealt with one who was the leader of His people. By personal subordination and intimate observation over a long period of time, Joshua was prepared for the mighty ministry which he later performed.

Elisha poured water on the hands of Elijah. 2 Kings 3:11. He followed him tenaciously. 2 Kings 2:1-13. By his fixed devotion to his master and concentration upon him, at last he became his heir.

The disciples of the Lord Jesus Christ turned into the way to follow Him many years before they were qualified to serve Him. By a day-by-day, night-by-night, year-in-and-year-out contact with Him, with a constant observance of His mighty works, sitting often at His feet, being trained, coached, and corrected by Him, by personal practice as they went out to preach and perform miracles in His name, coming back to report to their Master—by all of these things they received the experience which was most vital preparation for the ministry which they later performed.

These Bible examples demonstrate to us clearly that we need not expect other than a period of training and discipline before entering into full and effective ministry for our Lord. THERE IS NO SUBSTITUTE FOR EXPERIENCE! Brilliance and books are good in their places but the actual going over the road, the personal experience of doing the thing ourselves, is an absolute requisite in the development of skill and the acquiring of personal knowledge.

It cannot be truthfully denied that education makes its contribution to preparation for Christian ministry. The word *education* technically means a drawing out. This would imply that there is latent within each individual all possible qualification and capacity for life and service, and that these qualifications and capacities need drawing out or developing in order to become more effective. The word *education,* however, has come to denote an acquisition of knowledge as well. It is in both of these senses that we use the word.

Education is going to school. Formal education is attending institutions of learning—elementary, secondary, and higher. Informal education is attending the general school of life with personal application to books and other sources of knowledge. The acquisition of knowledge and the development of skill is that to which all ambitious-minded young people set themselves early in life. Our own government has decreed that democracy cannot endure if its citizens are illiterate. An eighth-grade education is the law of the state in America. This much education is not optional for us, and the individual who protests this law of the land for the mental training of his child is rare indeed. The continuation of grammar-school education into the upper grades of high school is likewise considered most desirable by the average parent and child. Where economic conditions allow, it is the practice of the American home that its children should go through high school. The difference between grammar and high school is only in extent and degree. The history, science, language, and arithmetic of the one are developed and advanced in the other.

There are those who hold that if grammar school is good and high school is better, a college education is simply a further step in the same direction. They hold that it is not more hurtful to spiritual life to study trigonometry than to study geometry; that it is no more harmful to spiritual qualities to study French and Spanish than to study the original Latin from which these languages sprang; that it is just as profitable to study the history of English literature as something of the literature itself; and just as good to study chemistry as to study physics. It is thought by some that a college education gives the equivalent in preparation for secular life today which high school provided twenty years ago; that a young person is no more qualified to secure a good position in the business world without a college education today than he would have been without a high-school education in the past generation. They feel likewise that attending college cannot be properly considered a violation of the laws of God or a declension from high spiritual standards, any more than the acquisition of a high-school or even a grammar-school education.

There are distinct advantages in having had a good secular education by way of preparation for effective ministry. There is no doubt that the minister must know how to study both his Bible and other books that pertain thereto. The ability to comprehend and retain what one reads is developed by long practice and study in the classroom. The laws of learning apply to theological books and the Bible itself as a book, as well as to the textbooks which one studies in school or college. To have learned these laws and to have practice in their operation is good training for study for effective ministry.

The knowledge of history which a comprehensive education includes also provides a rich field of illustration and confirmation of the eternal truths of the Christian religion. Beautiful expressions which have been coined by masters of language many times provide delightful vehicles of the truths which we wish to convey in gospel preaching. A knowledge of the various sciences provides not only an enlarged appreciation of the handiwork of God but marvelous illustrations of how He moves in the mysterious realm of spiritual activity. The knowledge of Greek and Hebrew opens up the original tongues in which the Blessed Book was written. It gives us shades of meaning and distinctions in thoughts which are not conveyed by any version or translation of the Bible however recent and improved.

To have such a well-rounded education, such a background of intellectual development, and an acquaintance with the liberal arts in general, gives one a poise in society which is a distinct advantage to a minister of the gospel. One does not have to pretend acquaintance with the matters being discussed by educated people, or cleverly to conceal one's ignorance, to say nothing of clumsily exposing such ignorance in cultured society. As advanced education is becoming more and more common our audiences will include better educated individuals, and there will be an obligation to minister to them as well as to others. Our lack of educational background will quickly disclose itself and a number in our audience may lose that natural respect for us which otherwise would have led to their listening attentively to our message.

There is nothing which lowers a minister of the gospel in the respect of his audience so quickly as to be guilty of gross breaches in English grammar. How often have those who have the dignity and position of a minister of the gospel and a preacher of the unsearchable riches of Christ made themselves appear quite ridiculous by outrageous violations of good speech. If the removal of these offenses is going to give us a more effective ministry for God, who can say that such removal will be detrimental in any wise? An educated man can minister to uneducated as well as to educated people, and the former will enjoy his speech whether they fully appreciate the excellence of it or not. They will also value association with those who are more educated than themselves, and will appreciate sitting under the ministry of such a one. The minister with very limited education is limited to minister to those of similar limitations. This gives the educated man a much broader ministry and makes him far better equipped, other things being equal.

Scriptural instances of men who were used of God, who had a good educational background, are to be found in Moses, Daniel, and Paul. Although Moses' education was not sufficient qualification for effective leadership by any possible means, yet his acquaintance with the general format of legislation and the common problems of administrative leadership doubtless provided acceptable grooves through which the Lord could flow with His divine revelation of the laws of God and with direction as to proper leadership of a large group of people. He was accustomed to a position of leadership by virtue of his natural training which made it easy for him to take the position and carry it gracefully at the call of God.

It was not an accident that Daniel was among those children in whom there was no blemish, but who were well favored and skillful in all wisdom and knowledge and understanding in science, and such as had ability to stand in the king's presence. Dan. 1:4. It was no accident that from this group he was chosen for further training and also for the spiritual revelations which later came to him. It is also recorded that God gave these four young men (Daniel, Shadrach, Meshach, and Abednego) knowledge and skill in all learning and wisdom, so that when the king inquired of them and they were examined of him he found them ten times better than all the magicians and astrologers that were in all his realm. Dan. 1:17-20. Here it is stated that God Himself gave them knowledge and skill in all learning and wisdom, even the kind that the king himself could understand and appreciate and that was required by him in a natural way as qualification to stand in his court. On this background of natural ability and secular education there came the revelation of dreams and visions, and the beautiful character and spiritual quality that Daniel had. His position as ruler over the whole province of Babylon, and as chief of the governors over all the wise men of Babylon, and as the senior of the three presidents of the 120 princes over the whole kingdom, placed him where he could exert tremendous influence for God—far more so than if he had held a lesser position. Of course, he could have used this glory for himself and feathered his own selfish nest, and thus have lost his opportunity for outstanding service for God; but he did not do so. He used his influence for a testimony for Jehovah, and so strong was he in that influence that the kings themselves were tremendously impressed and edicts were issued exalting the Lord God of Daniel.

Is it a mere coincidence also that, in addition to Moses as the outstanding law-giver and man of God in the Old Testament, there should come to us the example of Paul as the outstanding man of God in the New Testament? Although Paul's trust was not in excellence of speech or enticing words of man's wisdom, and he had learned to count all things but dross for the excellency of the knowledge of Christ Jesus the Lord, yet it was his trained mind through which the Lord came forth and gave to the world the marvelous revelation of the gospel of grace. Thus the outstanding men of the two Testaments were men of exceptional educational opportunities, but men who went on from such a position of advantage to the acquisition of spiritual qualities and power to complete their preparation for the exceptional ministries that the Lord gave to them.

But here it must be said in the words of the educated Paul himself that "not many wise men after the flesh, not many mighty, not many noble are called." 1 Cor. 1:26. "God hath chosen the foolish things of the world to confound the mighty." He forever insists that no flesh shall glory in His presence.

1 Cor. 1:27-29. "Where is the wise, where is the scribe, where is the disputer of this world? Hath not God made foolish the wisdom of this world?" Paul had learned this basic spiritual lesson, and came to the Corinthians and to others "not in excellency of speech or of wisdom, or with enticing words of man's wisdom." 1 Cor. 2:1-4. He would not use the wisdom of words lest the cross of Christ should be made of none effect. 1 Cor. 1:17. He had learned to surrender, to empty out and come to the end of his own ability, in order that the wisdom of God, the power of God, might operate and be manifest through him. This yieldedness on his part made it possible for God to impart unto him the knowledge of His will, in all wisdom and spiritual understanding. Col. 1:9. He had no confidence in the flesh or in his natural ability however good. His confidence was exclusively in the leadership of the Holy Spirit; his wisdom was not his own but that of Christ within and through him. His natural education can be considered as the wedge which had widened his own intellectual capacity, rather than the fountain from which flowed his knowledge, or the skill with which he operated for God.

Pride is an evil thing. Pride in education or pride in ignorance is equally evil. Pride is no respecter of persons and appears as often among the illiterate as among the well educated. It is pride that damns our souls and prevents God from blessing and using us.

[ 37 ]

"Knowledge indeed puffeth up" (1 Cor. 8:1), but knowledge that surrenders to God is more usable by Him than illiteracy.

Considering the general field of sacred education, we enter here upon a discussion that will not be in the nature of an argument. Who can deny, and who can dispute, that a knowledge of the Bible is absolutely essential in the way of preparation for Christian ministry? The Bible is the fountainhead of all spiritual truth and the revelation of the complete will of God. The preacher is the purveyor of spiritual truth and a channel through which that truth flows to the people. He must be attached to the fountainhead. He must be thoroughly familiar with the great cardinal doctrines of the Christian faith, with the precepts and the promises, and the great revelation of the plan and will of God. These are the things that he preaches. Concerning them the people will ask him. "For the priest's lips shall keep knowledge, and they shall seek the law at his mouth; for he is the messenger of the Lord of hosts." Mal. 2:7. The Bible is the Word of God bound in morocco. Jesus Christ is the Word of God in the flesh, the very fullness of the Godhead dwelling in Him bodily. "As we treat God's Word so we treat God Himself, and so at the last will God treat us."

To turn aside from one's original occupation and devote his entire time to the study of the Word of God as preparation for Christian ministry is exceedingly wise if he is in the position to do so. To refuse to listen to others who would teach us the Word of God, or to refuse to read the messages of others who have written with the same intent, is inconsistent and contrary to the Word of God and the Spirit of Christ. Such individuals who pose as the teachers of God's Word and expect others to listen to and be influenced by them are expecting from others that which they themselves are unwilling to practice. They refuse to be taught but ask their hearers to be taught. They refuse to listen to others but ask their hearers to listen to them. As the colored woman exclaimed, "Oh consistency, wheah you is?" God hath set in the church teachers, with divine ordination as such, and who hold that position in His divine economy. 1 Cor. 12:28; Eph. 4:11; Rom. 12:7. The Spirit of Christ never disobeys the Word of Christ, and as one is led by the Spirit of the Lord he will conform to the Word of the Lord in all its provisions. Christ Himself was taught of His Father. John 12:49 and 14:10. And blessed are they who can likewise be taught, for the Spirit of Christ is a teachable one. "And ye have no need that any man teach you" (1 John 2:27) is sometimes quoted as justification for individuals not receiving the teaching which could come to them through human channels. But John himself is here teaching those to whom he wrote and he would hardly be advising them to reject his own teaching. The Holy Spirit indwells the body of Christ and particularly those who have received "the anointing." "Ye have no need that any (natural) man teach you." In gospel work it is not the man that teaches us, even though it is a human teacher who stands before us or whose book we read. It is the Holy Spirit that is using a channel through which to teach us all things. May God give us grace and graciousness to be teachable and taught of Him through whatever instrument or channel He shall choose.

There are various methods by which the Bible may be studied. A general grasp of the facts of Bible history, from the creation of the world to the coming down of the new Jerusalem and the ushering in of the eternal state, are basic to further Biblical understanding. A synthetic comprehension of the Bible as a whole, with the relation of the various parts and books to each other, is also to be desired. There should follow also the analysis of each book with the grasp of its general character, its outstanding personalities, events and doctrines. A study of the cardinal doctrines of our faith likewise is very profitable. Dispensations and prophecy also will form an important part in our knowledge of Bible truth. The types of the Old Testament and the parables of the New are divinely created vehicles in which there come to us immortal truths. The Bible is a mine of infinite wealth, and blessed is the man that cries after knowledge and lifts up his voice for understanding, and seeks her as silver and searches for her as for hidden treasure. Prov. 2:2-5.

In addition to the Bible there are certain subjects which are closely allied and strongly contributory to effectiveness in Christian ministry. *Biblical Introduction* is the study of the history of our English Bible. In what languages was the Bible given originally? Where are the original or the oldest manuscripts? What about the various translations and versions? What is the comparative value of the authorized and the various revised versions of the present time? All of this is answered in the study of Biblical Introduction. Frankly, however, this is the science into which there crept the insidious evil formerly known as higher criticism. But it is not necessary that one should question the authorship and authenticity of any book in the Bible as he studies the history of its having been written and arranged in canon form. A reverent and profound conviction that the Bible is the Word of God and that every word therein is sound and true is sufficient to hold one throughout the study of Biblical Introduction.

*Christian Evidences* is one of the most thrilling of the subjects which a minister should follow in an all-round preparation for service. This is the study which brings out clearly the great wealth of proof which there is for the tremendous claims of Christianity. Jesus is the only begotten Son of God. The Bible is the revealed Word of God, written by God Himself as He moved upon holy men of old. Christianity is the only true religion and the only way to heaven. These claims can easily and abundantly be substantiated by the facts of history and science as well as by the miracle of the Word of God. These proofs will appeal even to the unregenerated man. How interesting and valuable is the story presented to us by Christian Evidences.

*Hermeneutics* is the science of interpretation. There are certain basic fundamental laws governing interpretation which when realized are self-apparent. A knowledge of these laws and a careful adherence thereto will save the Bible student from many extravagant and foolish interpretations of the Holy Word. It is well worth the time of any prospective minister to master the laws of Biblical Hermeneutics.

The term *Pastoral Theology* seems to be a misnomer. Theology is the study of God, and pastoral theology would possibly be "the pastor's own study of God," or "the study of God from a pastor's viewpoint." This is not the accepted meaning of the term "pastoral theology." It is meant to apply to the study of the art and science of being a pastor. Pastoral-ology, or the Science of Pastoral Work, would be better terms although not so euphonious. In any event, it is an alluring and most valuable study. The present textbook is a sample of the general field of thought covered by this subject. There are many phases of pastoral work and responsibility, and the study of this ministry is not only interesting but most important if one is contemplating such service.

Closely akin to the study of pastoral theology is

that of *Homiletics.* The pastor must preach, and homiletics teaches him how. There are various types of sermons, and a wrong and a right way to preach. This is a science which is essential for the preacher to know.

A knowledge of *Church History* likewise is a valuable background for Christian ministry. The various experiences of the Christian church, and the pitfalls into which she has fallen, serve as an excellent warning in the present-day condition of church affairs. One cannot afford to deny himself the advantage of the experience of the past as he is busy in making the present-day history of the church.

The study of *Personal Evangelism* is learning the various things needed in order to win souls to Christ. It is of great value to have this material to qualify Christians and especially Christian workers for successful soul-winning.

There are around us today many corruptions and counterfeits of the gospel which we preach. The prophets and apostles have warned us of the false teachers that should arise and deceive even the very elect if it were possible. The study of *Cultism* or Christian Polemics places the pastor in a position to warn his people and the public against the false teachers and preachers of our day.

Here we have seen in general what sacred education is. It is a study of the Bible, learning at the feet of teachers speaking or writing, and the comprehension of a general field of subjects that are auxiliary to a knowledge of the Bible and effective ministry. With this education sufficiently acquired, with at least a modest degree of secular education, and, above all things, with a knowledge of God and spiritual experiences of many kinds, the candidate for Christian service with a crystal-clear call to preach may consider himself moderately prepared for such ministry.

CHAPTER 3

# The Character of a Good Minister

A S the fruit of a tree is determined by the kind of tree it is, so all the ministry of a man of God will be influenced and controlled by the kind of man he is. The Lord Jesus said, "Out of the abundance of the heart the mouth speaketh." Matt. 12:34. The great preacher has it, "As he thinketh in his heart, so is he." Prov. 23:7. This requires that a man's heart shall be pure and full of the things that he wants to appear in his ministry. "Keep thy heart with all diligence, for out of it are the issues of life." Prov. 4:23. Jesus was full of grace and truth; and so, logically, that was what poured forth from His life. John 1:14.

In considering the character of a good minister, we shall note first of all certain natural traits that will be excellent and almost necessary for him to have. Natural traits are born in one by natural birth. But they are also capable of development and should be nourished and cultivated. Also it is good to know that, if certain traits seem to be entirely lacking, the wonderful grace of Jesus is such that we can acquire even these so-called "natural" traits at His great storehouse.

Foremost among these natural characteristics is *courage*. Our Master Himself was afraid neither of Herod nor of Pilate, nor of the whole Sanhedrin, nor of the howling mob that called for His blood, nor of Satan himself in the mount of temptation. When a mob was surging madly over the market place of Ephesus in defense of their goddess and in anger at the new preachers, Paul sought to go in among them. It was only the restraining of his friends and certain officials of the city which withheld him. Acts 19:30. Paul was bold in the presence of Felix, Festus, and Agrippa. Neither did he lack courage to speak boldly to Peter as occasion required. Gal. 2: 11-14.

This is a quality which will be sorely needed in a pastor's life. His ministry will have grave and unprincipled opposition. The devil is our sworn enemy and he will exhaust every means possible to thwart and undermine our work. He will stoop to any tactics and boldly and rudely oppose when he considers it timely. The pastor will be pushed around, snowed completely under, and eventually driven clear off the scene of action if he lacks the courage to stand out against the enemy. The opposition sometimes will come through carnal members of his own congregation. Error will try its hand at pressing in upon his flock. As little David arose in righteous anger to destroy the lion and the bear that threatened the lambs of his fold, so the man of God must be strong to resist the devil and stand in defense of his members. This courage should not be confused with ruthless force and high-handedness, for that is not what is meant. A love for sinners should accompany a hatred for sin. There must be the ability to distinguish a man from his deed. The strength of his courage must be tempered by the tenderness of his touch.

Another quality essential to a successful ministry is *diligence* or industry. We are told in Rom. 12:8, 11 that he that ruleth must do it with diligence, and that we should not be slothful in business. "Seest thou a man diligent in his business? He shall stand before kings." Prov. 22:29. Let no one think that the life of a pastor is a life of ease. It could be possible that some pastors themselves have this conception of their position. They are losing possibly one half of the opportunities which are theirs and will be held responsible in a commensurate degree. There is so much to be done in the way of spiritual ministry that there are hardly enough hours in the day and week in which to do it. He must replenish his own heart and mind day by day and also be busily engaged in the rescuing of precious souls, the upbuilding of his church, and the extension of the kingdom. This requires a consistent application from early morning till late at night. The layman works eight hours a day, and "a woman's work is never done." A man who has the responsibility of his business is never satisfied with a mere eight hours but spends every waking moment in intensive concentration upon the responsibilities of his task. This is the spirit and burden of a true man of God. There should be no streak of laziness in him, and every ounce of his energy and every moment of his time should be devoted endlessly to his tremendous task.

The quality of *dignity* should be found in the minister of the gospel. By this we do not refer to a stilted pietism, or a solemn mien which is sepulchral and forbidding, but we mean that calm self-control and dignified reserve which becomes one who is a leader of souls and who has such exceedingly important responsibilities resting upon him. Paul said to Timothy, "Let no man despise thy youth." 1 Tim. 4:12. To the saints at Ephesus he wrote that neither foolish talking nor jesting be found among them but rather giving of thanks. Eph. 5:4. The young preacher must restrain his boyishness and do nothing that would lower him in the esteem and respect of his flock and his townsmen. There should be no undue familiarity with those around him. That is to say, an intimacy which would be proper between those on the same social level or family relationship must not exist between him and the members of his congregation. They should not call him by his first name, and neither should he be similarly intimate and personal with them. He has the position of leadership by virtue of his office and should maintain it carefully if he is to be most effective in his work.

Not the least among the natural qualities which he should have and develop is *tact*. There are clumsy ways of doing the right thing which well-nigh defeat one's purpose. There cannot be a disregard of the principle of careful, considerate expression of one's thought and control of one's behavior without doing considerable damage to the cause of the Lord. In the matter, for instance, of rebuking disorder in the church, or in contradicting some statement which has been made publicly to which you cannot give the consent of your church, how careful one must be and how particular one's choice of words. Likewise the spirit in which the matter is said will influence the result and will help make his statement acceptable. Children can be called to order without creating resentment and their parents even can be made to smile. On the other hand, a severe cleavage may be wrought and sympathizers may be made for the offended one, if the pastor is artless and awkward in the manner in which he handles such a situation. We must do the difficult thing and "make them like it." Let no one consider that this is hypocritical and that being frank and outspoken is the better virtue to have. One can be tactful without being deceitful and we insist that being so is exceedingly wise.

*Discretion* is a quality which is of great value to a minister. We refer to conformity to the laws of propriety and the exercise of prudence on all occasions. The apostle Paul expresses it thus: "Let not your good be evil spoken of." Rom. 14:16. A perfectly innocent heart may carelessly put itself in a bad light and be falsely accused. Let a wise mind and firm will control the innocent heart. To be specific, all contacts with the opposite sex must be guarded most jealously. It is good to be a gentleman on all occasions. To assist the ladies in their need is the part of chivalry. But to conduct a lady to her home alone repeatedly could easily give rise to malicious gossip.

The apostle Peter enjoins his converts to be *courteous*. 1 Peter 3:8. Any professional man is expected to be a gentleman. All the more then should the leader of Christians and one who is classed with professional men be courteous and well mannered. The "please" and the "thank you" should never be missing, and commands should always be couched as requests. No rude intrusion into the conversations of others or the privacies of another's home should ever be laid at his door. The gracious touch and the winning smile, as well as the cultured refinement of a Christian gentleman, should always accompany the man of God.

In his personal attire he should be scrupulously *clean*. We do not say that he should be fastidious, or effeminate, but there should be a consistent cleanliness and neatness about his person and his attire. We are told in the Bible to "draw near with a true heart in full assurance of faith, having our hearts sprinkled from an evil conscience, and our bodies washed with pure water." Heb. 10:22. "Cleanliness is next to godliness" is sometimes mistakenly quoted as Scripture; however, it is thoroughly consistent with the Scriptures. There should be a cleanliness of mind and speech as well as that of the body. The pure mind will not make suggestive remarks, to say nothing of speaking of things which could not as well be spoken behind the sacred desk. The use of by-words and slang is unbecoming to a minister of the gospel. If his vocabulary needs strengthening let him learn more wholesome words, for there are sufficient in the English language. Our Lord Himself and also the apostle James tells us that our communications should be yea, yea, and nay, nay, and that whatsoever is more than these cometh of evil. Matt. 5:37; James 5:12.

*Punctuality* is a virtue. When an appointment is made and one's word is given, it is an obligation that has been entered into. To be late for an appointment, to say nothing of missing it altogether, is an injustice and wrong. It is annoying to those to whom we have given our word and it is a reflection upon our honesty as well as our precision of habits. It has been expressed that to be late for an appointment is to be a thief and a liar; we have stolen the other man's time and have been untrue to our word. Whenever such tardiness is unavoidable, proper apologies should be made. Never should a habit of carelessness in keeping appointments be acquired or reputation for such be developed.

Now let us consider the question of *leadership* and the elements involved therein. The consistent teaching of the New Testament presents the pastor as the spiritual leader of his people. The qualities of leadership therefore must be inherent in the pastor or developed as rapidly as possible. Leadership is not ruthless, as the domination of a slave driver. It is rather seniority which is instinctively recognized and respected for its wisdom and maturity. Leadership should not rest upon the authority of one's position but should rather be inherent in the quality of one's ability and character  Recognition of this leadership should be instinctive and sincere, and without compulsion or constraint. To lead a group of men, one should be out in front. That is to say, he should be farther down the road than those whom he is leading. He should be going in the same direction and have gone farther and have done more and have become more capable than those who follow him.

Involved in this principle of leadership is a willingness to assume responsibility. Decisions will have to be made; and although it is safe not to risk becoming responsible for a decision, yet this quality is inherent in leadership. One must weigh the issues carefully, pray through, and then have the courage to make a definite decision. This willingness to assume responsibility will be expected of a pastor.

Executive ability is included in this consideration and should be found in good measure in the leader of a church. This quality calls for discrimination as to the various tasks which need to be done in connection with the whole church program, the arranging and proper grouping of these tasks according to their relative importance, the wise choice of workers to discharge them, and the tactful assignment to duties. There must then follow the efficient supervision of these workers, their encouragement and assistance, and possible replacement as occasion requires. "It is far better to put ten men to work than to attempt to do the work of ten men," has been wisely said. Executive ability will result in much more being done for God and a happier and more efficient church in every way. This is surely a quality which is at high premium and which can be considered one of the most important.

Leadership also involves a knowledge of human nature. This comes by instinct, observation, and experience. It should not take us long to learn that people balk when they are commanded, and that they resent attacks and will surely fight back. On the other hand, they respond to compliments and kindness and a sincere interest in their personal welfare. It will be well to become acquainted with other intricacies in human reactions and a knowledge of them will be useful as a means to the great end of getting our gospel into the hearts and homes of the people.

Now we come to the realm of *spiritual* qualifications and characteristics. Immediately we are face to face with the Son of God who is the consummate embodiment of all these virtues—love, faith, holiness, humility, patience, and a forgiving spirit.

Love of God can mean a love for God and also God's love within the heart. In both these senses a minister's heart should be full of *the love of*

*God.* Loving the Lord his God with all his heart, soul, mind, and spirit is his first duty. As this is done, consecration will be complete. There will be no chafing or resentment at any feature of his life and ministry. As the one whom he loves has called him and his love for Him remains strong and true, then every question is answered and all is well. This is very important and is the solution of all personal problems. God Himself is love and we just need more of God when our love runs short.

In a similar way it takes a full measure of God's love to enable us to minister effectively to the people. Human nature generally is ungrateful, selfish, and unkind. There may be lack of appreciation of our sacrifice and effort. Our natural love will soon run out and we will turn against those to whom we are sent and to whom we minister. The great overflowing love of God within our hearts will cause us to love the unlovely and the unlovable, will make us do good to them that despitefully use us, and cause us to continue to pour out our lives on behalf of those who are unworthy and who may even do us personal injustices. Here is a quality that must fill one's heart if one is to succeed in a pastorate or on the missionary field.

Closely akin to love and almost as important in Christian life and service is the quality of *faith*. From the beginning to the end of the Christian life, faith is the key that unlocks the treasures of God. By faith we are saved. By faith we are kept. By faith we receive the Baptism of the Holy Spirit. The just shall live by faith, and without faith it is impossible to please God. By faith likewise we, like Enoch, shall be caught up to meet the Lord when He comes. All of the work which a preacher must perform is of the supernatural kind. Who can save a human soul? Who can change men's minds and hearts? Who can effect a supernatural healing of the body? Who can baptize in the Holy Spirit? Who can break down prejudice and make enemies do that which they would not? Only God can do these things. But the preacher too must do them. How can he do them? By moving God to bring them to pass. Faith is the power that moves God; hence faith is absolutely essential to a successful ministry.

How can one preach *holiness* and lead others into a life of holiness if he does not live a holy life? "Be ye clean that bear the vessels of the Lord." Isa. 52:11. Without holiness, no man shall see the Lord. Heb. 12:14. A poor demonstration of the power of his gospel is the preacher who does not exemplify in his life the power of God to make one holy. If he himself does not practice what he preaches it is definite proof of his insincerity in preaching, and turns his message aside as worthless, professional, and hypocritical. A sense of justice and the rightness of things makes even people on the street demand that a preacher shall be true to his word, shall be pure in mouth, shall be honest in all his dealings, and shall live a clean, holy life. Of course, this is altogether possible or else our whole presentation of divine truth is wrong. "His power can make you what you ought to be." His grace is sufficient for us.

The enemy has a way of defiling a holy life which he cannot besmirch otherwise by sowing the tares of pride while men sleep. Subtly and without perception or detection, this wicked leaven begins its deadly work and ere long there is unmistakable evidence of spiritual pride. Then too there are the common varieties of pride—pride of profession, pride of position, and pride of place. To be the "minister" gives little souls the big-head. Their position is such that they will not soil their hands in any manual labor around the church. They are inclined to be officious and resentful of any challenge to their authority or any brooking of their power. How pathetic and ruinous is such an attitude, and how utterly it disqualifies one to be a spiritual leader of spiritual men. "Take My yoke upon you, and learn of Me, for I am meek and lowly of heart." "And He took a towel and girded Himself, and began to wash His disciples' feet." "I have given you an example, that ye should do as I have done to you." "Mind not high things, but condescend to men of low estate. Be not wise in your own conceits." *Humility* is as important as it is rare.

Works of great importance and of enduring worth are not accomplished in a short time. A chicken coop can be built in an hour or so but a magnificent temple requires years to erect. The work of God in a church or community is in reality the building of a holy temple which will be a habitation of God through the Spirit.  Nothing on earth can compare in value or in enduring quality to that spiritual building which the man of God is erecting.  The farmer "waiteth for the precious fruit of the earth, and hath long patience for it, until he receive the early and the latter rain."  The seed of the Word will need time for its germination, growth, and maturity.  The pastor must stand patiently by and faithfully do his part and await the growth and development which, although imperceptible, is in process.  Thus *patience* too is a spiritual quality with which ministers of the Word and workers in the harvest field must be endowed.  1 Thess. 5:14.

As long as human nature runs true to form there will be occasions when one will have to exercise a *forgiving spirit*.  If an offence comes and a grudge is held, then a schism has begun which will seriously hurt if not absolutely disrupt.  A pastor cannot expect that his people should be more Christlike than he himself.  It takes two to make a quarrel and, if the pastor will take the initiative in overlooking and forgiving a wrongdoing, then he is the better Christian as he should be.  If he cannot arise to the demand upon his spiritual character, and succumbs to carnality, resentment, and retaliation, it spells defeat for him and means the end of his usefulness in the ministry.  How glorious to be able to take the sweet spirit of Him who said, "Father, forgive them, for they know not what they do!"  If Stephen and Paul were able to reflect and exemplify this spirit of forgiveness (Acts 7:60; 2 Tim. 4:16), then surely it is possible for present-day gospel workers to manifest forgiveness. Eph. 4:32.

There are many distractions to one called of God into gospel ministry. If the enemy cannot stop or retard, he will attempt to deflect. Inducements may be offered to procure additional income and a measure of natural satisfaction by an occupation on the side. Our Master has told us that if our eye be single our whole body shall be full of light. "No man can serve two masters. Ye cannot serve God and mammon." Matt. 6:22-24. The apostle Paul expressed the same warning in this language: "No man that warreth entangleth himself with the affairs of this life, that he may please Him who hath chosen him to be a soldier." 2 Tim. 2:4. It is not only a diversion but a distinct distraction if one is occupied with his left hand in material, earthly money-making and attempts with the other to do full-fledged gospel work. Are we not told, "Having food and raiment let us be therewith content"? The love of money may cause one to err from the faith, to be pierced through with many sorrows, and to be drowned at last in destruction and perdition. 1 Tim. 6:8-10. This comment is not intended to rebuke or discourage those who make a living on the side in order that they may preach the gospel. This is most commendatory and in many home mission ventures is absolutely necessary. However, when a church is developed sufficiently to provide even a meager income, it is far better to launch out in faith and devote one's whole time to gospel work. The church will profit immediately by this increased attention, and God and the people will respond toward the support of the worker who trusts God and loves souls in such an heroic fashion.

There is one more spiritual quality which we shall mention here. It is possible for a devout church worker to become so involved and so burdened with the tasks and responsibilities which are his that he will become bowed down and laden with care. This is going a little too far. After all, the work is His. The responsibility likewise is His if we do our part well. The government must be upon His shoulders. He has distinctly commanded us to cast all our care upon Him for He cares for us. 1 Peter 5:7. Paul expresses it, "I would have you without carefulness." 1 Cor. 7:32. There is a carefreeness and joy and victory of soul which should characterize the step, song, spirit, and whole attitude of a minister of the gospel. God is on the throne. His is a wonderful gospel story. We have the high honor of being His messengers, and why shouldn't we be happy and carefree?

# CHAPTER 4

## The Minister in His Private Life

THERE is no realm of the minister's life into which the light of God should not shine. Truly there is nothing hidden from Him with whom we have to do. Heb. 4:13. It is impossible for a minister to be truly spiritual in public and carnal in private. There must be a constant and consistent spiritual quality in every phase of his life. It is therefore not only permissible but proper that we look into the minister's private life, in addition to considering the problems which have to do with his public ministry.

"O Lord, I know that the way of man is not in himself. It is not in man that walketh to direct his steps." Jer. 10:23. "In all thy ways acknowledge Him and He shall direct thy paths." Prov. 3:6. This eternal law applies to every problem in a person's life. We are absolutely unable to find "the way of life" by our own wisdom or the light of our own counsel. But God has not left man alone. He has provided for him personal guidance in all matters if man will avail himself of the divine instrument which is proferred him. Now if this applies to every detail and every decision of life, how much more must it apply to the great question of choosing a life companion. Abraham Lincoln and John Wesley are outstanding examples of the tremendous handicap a man must suffer if unhappily married. How careful then must we be to be sure that we are led of the Lord in the matter of matrimony. For those who are unmarried there comes the command, "Seek not a wife." 1 Cor. 7:27. On the other hand, the Bible declares, "Whoso findeth a wife findeth a good thing and obtaineth favor of the Lord." Prov. 18:22. The harmony between these two scriptures is that we should leave the matter of a companion entirely in the hands of the Lord who knows our need. We must have His definite guidance in the choice of a life companion. When such is provided for us by the Lord Himself we have indeed gotten a good thing and obtained favor of the Lord. It will hardly be necessary to say to prospective ministers or missionaries that it is definitely un-Scriptural to be yoked together with unbelievers. 2 Cor. 6:14. This is an eternal law which applies to all Christians and which if broken will bring no end of misery and woe.

There are distinct advantages in being married. God has said that it is not good that man should be alone. Gen. 2:18. The human heart craves companionship. One's nature is not complete or well rounded within itself for God has ordained that two shall constitute one complete whole. Matt. 19:6.

To be able to unburden one's heart to another and to be conscious of the fact that there is another sharing all the problems of life is a satisfaction to the human heart. The Lord Himself sent His disciples out two and two (Luke 10:1), thus endorsing the principle of companionship in Christian service. The great preacher has told us that two are better than one, for if one fall the other will lift up his fellow. Eccl. 4:9-12.

Another advantage is that of counsel. No man is sufficient within himself in the way of wisdom and good judgment. How fortunate to have another to present a different viewpoint in order that a balanced conception of the situation may be obtained. Just to have one with whom to talk over a certain problem is in itself an advantage, for the verbal expression of ideas enables one to see the matter from a better viewpoint and to arrive at a better conclusion. The advice received by the other is many times the very thing needed. It is good for one spiritually to take counsel from another for it lowers our self-sufficiency and cultivates humility and teachableness. Another advantage of being married is that one's natural life is thereby completed. It enables us to enter into the joys and sorrows and the many complications of human experience for better if we ourselves are partaking of these experiences.

There is one modification, however, which should be mentioned in connection with the advantages of being married. We are warned by the apostle Paul in 1 Cor. 7:33 that "he that is married careth for the things that are of the world, how he may please his wife." 1 Cor. 7:33. It is natural and proper that a husband should be a good provider and should devote his earnings to the welfare and benefit of his wife and children. In the natural and the merely human, this is the highest duty of his life and is most wholesome and proper. For a minister, however, this must not be uppermost. The Lord Himself has declared: "If any man come to Me and hate not his father, and mother, and wife, and children, and brethren, and sisters, yea, and his own life also, he cannot be My disciple." Luke 14:26. There must be a subordination of our homes and our loved ones to the great and supreme call of God on our lives. To Christians in general this applies, it is true, but it applies all the more to ministers who must constantly be upon God's altar in material, domestic matters as well as in all others. The pastor and his wife must hold very loosely all the material possessions that God has given them. One should never be "married" to a pastorate, parsonage, neighborhood, or certain climate. Material things must be kept altogether subordinate to the great spiritual objective of the highest will of God. With the pastor and his wife there must be a mutual subordination of material things which will amount to an actual renunciation of all things earthly for God. Our children likewise must be upon this same altar. We must give anything and go anywhere and at any time according to His will. But, after all, this is a life of supreme joy and our heavenly Father will see that if we seek first the kingdom of God and His righteousness all these things shall be added unto us.

"They made me a keeper of the vineyards; but my own vineyard have I not kept." This was the cry of the bride in the Song of Solomon. 1:6. But it can also be the sad confession of some pastors and their wives in connection with their own children. This is not to be commended but rather to be deplored. If a man is a pastor and father, he must not forget the latter in his emphasis on the former. Our attention to spiritual matters and the welfare of others, however great, can never atone or compensate for ignoring our responsibility to our own children. If a man has taken to himself a wife and God has blessed that union with children, then here is a responsibility which is definite and certain and from which there is no escape. A pastor is a Christian parent even though a pastor, and must discharge his duty fully as such. He is as obligated as any man within his assembly to train his children and to provide for them.

It is the will of God that a pastor and his wife shall set up and conduct a home which shall be a pattern for the believers. Titus 2:7. Our people are going to follow our example more than they will obey our precepts. Regardless of our desires in the matter, they will certainly observe how our households are conducted and may even be free to make comments concerning it. The only feature of this situation that we can change is to provide them good

[ 64 ]

material upon which to comment. Our heavenly Father has a Son for whom a bride is being prepared. He conducts His household as a pattern for all His children, being full of mercy and being true to His own eternal laws. The pastor likewise in his parish must conduct his household as an example to the members of his church. How beautiful a way in which to preach the gospel and to demonstrate its beauty and worth! If a man fails in this opportunity and obligation he does so to his distinct discredit, and cripples himself greatly in his effectiveness as a pastor.

The qualifications for the ministry as set forth in 1 Tim. 3:4-5 declare that he must "rule well his own house having his children in subjection with all gravity; for if a man know not how to rule his own house, how shall he take care of the church of God?" Here is a distinct and definite command to ministers regarding the conduct of their homes, a specific instruction of the Bible concerning this matter. The Lord Himself has put His finger upon this need and is calling our attention to it.

We have some outstanding examples in the Bible about how God has taken His own commands very seriously in this regard. Eli was a good man and as far as the record goes was himself not guilty of any wrongdoing in the discharge of his official duties. However, his sons were wicked, and because of his failure to govern his household and control his sons, he was deposed and his sons were slain. A calamity came to him because "his sons made themselves vile and he restrained them not." 1 Sam. 3:13. On the other hand, the Lord smiled upon Abraham, declaring, "I know him, that he will command his children and his household after him, and they shall keep the way of the Lord, to do justice and judgment." Gen. 18:19. It seemed that the Lord was rather proud of Abraham and certainly rewarded him for the control which he had over his own household. It is the will of God that all children should be subordinate to their parents and that all fathers should bring them up in the nurture and admonition of the Lord. Eph. 6:1-4. How much more so must the pastor himself and his children be obedient to these commands. The minister's children, as specifically declared in Titus 1:6, must be faithful and live such exemplary lives that even the accusation of being unruly could not be laid against them. This is a high standard but the Lord Himself has set it for His ministers.

Concerning the care of the body, which is also a part of one's private life, there are certain things for us to remember. Our spirits and souls are resident within our bodies. We may be thoroughly consecrated and equipped spiritually and mentally, but if our bodies are ill or incapacitated our whole beings are rendered impotent. Our bodies are the vehicles in which our whole ministry rides. A breakdown in the vehicle will delay the arrival and completely thwart and nullify all other preparation and ability. It is therefore reasonable for us to take good care of the bodies that the Lord has given us. Our bodies are the temples of the Holy Ghost (1 Cor. 6:19, 20) and bodily exercise profits a little. 1 Tim. 4:8. To have a splendid physique is no end within itself and is a small accomplishment from a spiritual standpoint, but for the devoted, consecrated minister to have a good physique is a tremendous advantage. It will enable him to expend himself for God and to give full expression and effectiveness to his spiritual and mental capacities.

For a minister to abuse his body is just as foolish as for anyone else to do so. Nature always collects. If we attempt such a multitude of duties that our bodies have little time for relaxation or recuperation, then we need not be surprised if there comes a breakdown of our health. Psalm 127:2 states, "It is vain for you to rise up early, to sit up late, to eat the bread of sorrows; for so He giveth His beloved sleep." Jesus told His disciples, "Come apart and rest a while." Mark 6:31. A modern evangelist phrased it thus: "If we don't come apart and rest, we will simply come apart." Intensive ministry is the will of God for us all. Diligence and industry should characterize our work all the way through. Idleness and slothfulness lie under God's condemnation. But it is certainly not the part of wisdom nor the will of God that we should abuse the bodies that He has given us. Our bodies can be hurt and our physical health and spiritual effectiveness impaired by the habit of overeating. Jesus warned that we should not be overcharged with surfeiting (overeating) and

[ 67 ]

so that day come upon us unawares. Luke 21:34. A certain servant, said He, would give himself to eating and drinking and say, "My Lord delayeth His coming," and be cut off for so doing. Matt. 24: 48-51. Temperance (self-control) is a fruit of the Spirit (Gal. 5:23), and Paul knew how to "keep his body under." 1 Cor. 9:27. Overeating is a self-indulgence which does not become a preacher of the self-denying gospel of our Lord Jesus Christ. On the other hand, prolonged fasting, too often repeated, can likewise affect our health and the enemy of our souls can thus take advantage of us.

It is the part of wisdom for a pastor to budget his time. As a man goes to his meals and to his business according to a regular schedule, so it is wise that a pastor shall make out a schedule for himself and adhere thereto as closely as possible. It is human nature to put off an unpleasant matter as long as we can. It is also natural to choose the most delightful things first of all. As a child at the table, if unrestrained, will take his dessert first to the ruination of his appetite and digestion, so the preacher, if he has no control over his time, will choose the most delightful and easy things to do and as a result usually exclude the things that would have been to his mental and spiritual advantage and discipline.

Let no minister allow himself more time for sleep than that which he allows the men of his church the morning after the service the previous night. It is hardly fair to expect his people to remain for long after-services and get up early the next morning when he and his evangelist sleep late. The pastor should be a laborer as well as they, and should have only the amount of sleep which is common to man. Let him arise and go about his daily duty as early and as regularly as the others of his congregation. Prov. 6:9-11.

It is most convenient that a minister should devote his mornings to prayer and study. This is the time of day when visiting is least in order. Likewise it is the hour when one's mind is freshest and most able to study and pray. As Peter said in Acts 6:4, it is the part of wisdom that a minister shall give himself continuously to prayer and the ministry of the Word. There should be the daily devotional period first of all. This is the reading of the Scriptures for food and private prayer for spiritual welfare. This is as vital to spiritual health as material food is to physical health. How utterly foolish for ministers to consider that they can survive by merely inhaling the spiritual food which they serve to others or by observing it as they wait upon God's tables. Every restaurant waiter must partake of food as well as handle it daily, and every preacher must partake for his own spiritual betterment as well as serve others continually to this end. It is a subtle temptation to consider that one can live by spiritual atmosphere alone. A camp meeting is a good place to backslide if one neglects private prayer and devotion! Bible

School or pastoral work also has witnessed some spiritual shipwrecks for the same reason.

It is suggested that ministers have a regular plan of Bible reading for their private devotions rather than reading promiscuously. If we follow no rule in our reading, we will unconsciously seek just those scriptures that have been a blessing to us in times past and that appeal to us as most full of spiritual truth. This will result in vast areas of the Word of God going altogether unexplored. We are told in 2 Tim. 3:16 that all Scripture is given by inspiration of God and is profitable. Why limit ourselves to certain portions or to certain kinds of food when we can have the delightful variety which God's Word affords? As a balanced diet, with its proper proportion of proteins, starches, fats and sweets, contributes to our physical health, so a wide and diversified reading of what God has provided in His Word will be a great blessing to us spiritually. The reading of the entire Bible through every year is the minimum which a preacher should have as his goal. If regular church members should do this (and they should), how much more should ministers, who need constant replenishing in their spiritual lives even more than others. Prayer will precede or follow the reading of the Word or be interspersed through it according to one's own impulse. How blessed to be conscious of the presence of the Lord throughout our entire devotional period. Through His Word He speaks to us and through our words we speak to Him. Beautiful, blessed communion with the Lover of our souls!

Following the devotional period, there can be the study of the Bible and kindred books and other related reading. This will be considered in detail in a later chapter. Break the intensity of the morning study once, if necessary, by a brief recess or relaxation, but on the whole reserve your mornings for prayer and study.

The afternoons can well be spent in pastoral visitation. At least four days a week should be spent in this way. The various features of this type of ministry will be discussed in a later chapter. "Off nights" can be occupied to great advantage in the visitation of men who are unavailable through the day. A pastor's time will be fully occupied in the beautiful work to which God has called him. Surely he must redeem the time, because the days are evil. Eph. 5:16.

It will be well to have a weekly schedule to provide for variation from day to day. *Sunday* is the all-important day and must be thoroughly prepared for in advance. Some ministers prefer to use Monday as a day of preparation for the following Sunday, while others wait till Saturday. Whatever the inclination along this line, there should be *one entire day* at least devoted to preparation for the intense ministry which comes to us on each Lord's Day. Considering the truth stated in a paragraph above concerning the health of one's body, it can be accepted as proper that *one entire day* be set aside for physical and mental rest and relaxation. God Himself rested on the seventh day after His work of six days. The proportion of one day of rest out of seven is thus according to His precedent as well as His divine precept. Ex. 20:9. This would result in the refreshing of the entire being and doubtless enable one to accomplish as much in the six remaining days as could have been done in the entire seven had work been unbroken. The law of the tithe teaches us that God's blessing is upon the nine tenths so that it has a greater purchasing power than the ten tenths would have had if God were ignored. Possibly this same law obtains in connection with the day of rest.

Finally let it be said that a schedule must be considered as a servant rather than a master. There will arise occasions when a schedule must be broken into because of the exigencies of the case. There will be funerals on some afternoons and visits which have to be made some mornings. But let these variations be exceptions only and hold as closely as possible to the general rule.

# CHAPTER 5

# The Minister's Wife

"AND the king said unto me (the queen also sitting by him)." Neh. 2:6. "To him that overcometh will I grant to sit with Me in My throne, even as I also overcame and am set down with My Father in His throne." Rev. 3:21. It is proper that thrones should be shared. It is the divine pattern and is sometimes followed on earth that there should be a queen as well as a king. In pastoral work, the pastor is the ruler of his church. It is proper and complete that his wife should be co-ruler with him. His own queen is the queen of the parsonage, and of the pastorate too. When a ruler is alone in his ruling, he can easily become autocratic. This extreme the Lord has warned against in His Word. 1 Peter 5:3. A proper safeguard and balance in this connection is a consultant and advisor in the form of a wife who shares not only his home but the responsibility of his ministry.

The relationship which a pastor sustains to his

wife is similar to that which exists between God the Father and God the Son. In John 10:30 Jesus said: "I and My Father are one." He stated in John 14:28, "My Father is greater than I." Both of these statements are true. There is the sense in which God the Father and God the Son are co-equal but it is also to be observed that, as regards final authority and seniority, the Father is greater than the Son. And yet, where is there any conflict between them? Each loves the other and spends Himself on behalf of the other. John 17:24; 14:31. "The Father loveth the Son and showeth Him all things that Himself doeth." John 5:20. "All things that the Father hath are Mine." John 16:15. On the other hand, the Son did always the things that pleased the Father. John 8:29; 12:49. Here is the beautiful and perfect example of partnership in love and leadership, yet with the provision that in some senses one is greater than the other.

There is a reason why it is necessary that one of two should be indicated as the greater. If there should be a difference of opinion between the two and the two were equal in every regard then there would merely be a stalemate and a tie, with no provision made for the breaking of that tie. Hence for the sake of united action and effective government, a provision must be included giving a certain one the final word of decision. This need not in any wise interfere with the equality and love which exists between them. The right to make the final decision is counterbalanced by the additional responsibility.

In the case of God the Father and our Lord Jesus Christ it would never dawn upon one that Christ was less to be esteemed than His Father. As a matter of fact, Christendom would sooner be guilty of exalting the Son more than the Father if there were any distinction to be made in the Godhead. But the exaltation of Christ is "to the glory of God the Father." Phil. 2:11.

This serves as a divine pattern and example of the proper relationship between husband and wife. In a very true sense they are one. "For this cause shall a man leave father and mother, and shall cleave to his wife; and they twain shall be one flesh. Wherefore they are no more twain, but one flesh. What therefore God hath joined together, let no man put asunder." Matt. 19:5, 6. This reciprocity of love, devotion, honor, and confidence is patterned after that which exists between the Father and the Son. There should never be a question of division between them any more than there is between the persons of the Godhead; but, as with our illustration, God has ordained that the final decision in any matter shall rest with the man of the household. "But I would have you know that the head of every man is Christ, and the head of the woman is the man, and the head of Christ is God." 1 Cor. 11:3. The man in turn is subordinate to Christ, and Christ Himself to the Father. The woman is not inferior to the man, for in many respects she is the more loved of the two. The children cling to mother's skirts more readily than they do to father's knee. Being relieved of the responsibility of making the final decision is a protection to the woman, and an honor. As our civilization assigns men to war and to the hard work of the day, protecting its women out of respect and love for them, so God has laid upon man the burdens and responsibility of the decisions of life as a shield for the woman and out of respect for her.

The pastor's wife is a Christian wife first of all, and as such plays the role of a Christian wife and mother. The Word declares in Eph. 5:22-24, "Wives, submit yourselves unto your own husbands, as unto the Lord. For the husband is the head of the wife, even as Christ is the head of the church: and He is the savior of the body. Therefore as the church is subject unto Christ, so let the wives be to their own husbands in every thing." The substance of this injunction is repeated in Col. 3:18; Titus 2:4, 5; 1 Tim. 2:9-15; 1 Peter 3:1-6.

Our consideration here is of the wife of a Christian worker. In a very true and definite sense it can be said that the pastor's wife can make or break her husband. She stands at his side so closely and is in such intimate relationship to him that she knows and can touch his vulnerable parts at will. As a wrestler knows the places of the human body which are particularly vital and easily liable to injury, so it is given unto a wife to be in a position to influence her husband most vitally and tremendously. She can shield him in his weakest parts or attack him there, according to her choice. She is with him in his moments of discouragement and despair. She stands at his side as he faces his greatest temptation. She knows the struggle of his mind and heart. With her is the power to administer the comfort, encouragement, and help in obtaining divine strength and stamina, on the one hand; or to tilt the scales in a fleshly natural direction, causing him to break under the strain and to make a choice away from God. What an opportunity and responsibility is hers!

How great is the sin and the failing of the pastor's wife who influences her husband in a carnal direction. Does she not know that his failure is hers, or that his spiritual success is hers? She is one with him for better or for worse, and rises or falls with him. It would seem as though from sheer self-interest she would influence him to make that decision which would be to the credit of them both. But all too often her eyes are blinded with carnal reasoning and her bosom surges with purely natural emotion. The fireman who rides in the locomotive cab along with the engineer knows that he will be hurled to death along with him if the train leaves the track; so the wife ought to realize that if she puts her hand upon the throttle and diverts the spiritual progress of the preacher she will ruin herself as well as her husband.

Bible history carries illustrations of the truths which we here teach. There was a man in the land of Uz who was perfect and upright, one that feared God and eschewed evil. He had a wife who stood at his side. Reverses came; calamities befell him; he lost all his possessions and finally his health. The wife at his side, although the mother of his children and the keeper of his home, failed him at this crucial hour. "Then said his wife unto him, Dost thou still retain thine integrity? Curse God and die." Job 2:9. The last straw was thus laid upon him by way of pressure. His last stronghold was swept away, and the one whom he had chosen as his helpmeet failed to help him; she even turned upon him in attack. This was the uttermost by way of crucial testing, the refining of his deepest soul. But Job was a man after God's own heart, and he stood the test and retained his integrity. "But he said unto her, thou speakest as one of the foolish women speaketh." Job 2:10. She had an opportunity to assist him, to be a true wife to him in the fullest sense. She failed him and God, and became a liability rather than an asset.

Notice here that although Job was entitled to the support of his wife, yet he would not have been justified had he failed God when that support was denied him. Unlike Adam, he did not have to report a failure to God with the alibi, "The woman Thou gavest me . . . " If he was to be denied the consolation and encouragement of the wife of his bosom, he would nevertheless refuse to sell his soul and do that which was wrong. What a striking example of stalwart Christian integrity and manhood is this! Men and pastors are normally entitled to the love and support of their wives. But if this is denied them it is still demanded of them that they walk humbly and faithfully with God and, though the whole world turn against them, be true to the last. A woman who taunts her husband and goads him with stinging epithets, challenging him to "be a man and do his duty," meaning to fight his opponents in a carnal way or to resign the ministry to provide her the money that she wants, is the worst enemy that a man can have and withal the hardest to overcome. But he must not fail nevertheless. God blamed Adam and punished him severely for his share in the sin and for his weakness in yielding to his wife's inducement. May God grant that if the crisis comes in the lives of Christian ministers, they will stand with the integrity of Job and not fail with the weakness of Adam.

Another instance of the "liability wife" is that of Lot. We do not have the details of the family consultations when Lot looked upon the well-watered plains and chose them. We would not therefore be right in saying that his wife had a part in that choice, if it were not for the revelation of the condition of her heart at the end. Without a doubt her affections were in Sodom. She longed for it even though she was leaving it. Her other daughters were there. All her earthly possessions were there, and where her treasures were there her heart was also. It may have been that she influenced her husband to make that choice to live in Sodom in the first place, for there her daughters would have social opportunities and she herself could have the material comforts of a modern home rather than the roughness of tent life in the mountains. Lot succumbed to her petitions and, although the wickedness of the city vexed his righteous soul from day to day, he nevertheless remained there, possibly at the dictum of his wife. He might as well have refused her in the first place, for he lost her in the end, and his weakness of character has branded him forever as an inferior type of believer.

A very refreshing example of how a wife bolstered and strengthened her husband is that of Manoah and his wife in connection with the birth of the baby Samson. The angel appeared to her with a revelation of the coming event. She immediately told her husband and he instructed her to let him know if the angel appeared to her again. Upon the reappearance of the angel she immediately informed her husband as he had requested and together they prepared a sacrifice for the angel. As the angel did wondrously and ascended in the flame of fire from the altar, Manoah was terror-stricken. "We shall surely die because we have seen God. But his wife said unto him, If the Lord were pleased to kill us He would not have received a burnt offering and a meat offering at our hands, neither would He have showed us all these things, nor would as at this time have told us such things as these." Judges 13:22, 23. With old-fashioned common sense, she bolstered her husband, and encouraged him not to be afraid but to believe God for the fulfilment of the promise. How fortunate is the pastor whose wife encourages and comforts his heart when it seems that the burden is too heavy to bear. She reminds him of the unfailing presence of the Lord and the certainty of the reward which is theirs if they carry on faithfully for God. How sweet and wonderful are these godly women to pay the full price of self-sacrifice in limitations as regards earthly possessions and popularity in order to take the rugged pathway with Christ and their Christian husbands. Great shall be their reward in heaven.

A lack of consecration with disastrous effects for her husband and her children is written at the very top of the human record in the story of Mother Eve. She disbelieved God, believed Satan, and straightway led her husband in the pathway of disobedience. Gen. 3:6. What a glaring example of the disaster of such a procedure she has set for all her daughters. Miriam was a prophetess. Today she would be recognized as an ordained minister of the gospel. She nevertheless manifested distinct carnality in her personal criticism of her pastor brother, Moses. God's wrath immediately fell upon her. Surely He is no respecter of persons. His wrath will fall upon all who manifest carnality. God is also the silent listener to every conversation. Even though Miriam and Aaron spoke in privacy the conviction of their heart concerning Moses' actions, yet God heard and God was angry. "Come out ye three unto the tabernacle of the congregation." And Miriam was punished with leprosy because of her sin.

If the Lord has given children to a pastor's wife, she must realize her obligation to them. Moses' mother was a godly woman and trusted God for the protection of her child. Heb. 11:23. Surely it is the prerogative of a godly mother to love, train, and teach her children. Titus 1:6; 2:4; Prov. 22:6. She shares with her husband the responsibility of conducting her household in that way that will be in accord with God's law and thus an example to the members of their assembly. She has equal opportunity and commensurate responsibility for the creation and maintenance of a godly home that will serve as a pattern to the believers. Although properly interested in the spiritual welfare of every child of the church, she must remember her first duty to her own children. No amount of public work or official duties will be considered a compensation and counterbalance for any neglect which she may show her own children. If the issue arises which requires that she make a decision between her duty to her children and public ministry that may be offered her, and she finds it impossible to take care of both, it is her bounden duty to be true to her own children first.

When it comes to the realm of the wife's relation to her husband's church, in some senses they stand co-equal and co-responsible. In Christ Jesus there is neither male nor female. Gal. 3:28. The Bible clearly presents the woman as a gospel worker as well as the man. Philip the evangelist had four daughters which did prophesy. Acts 21:9. The very first news of the resurrection was committed to women to tell. Matt. 28:5, 10. "Phoebe our sister" was the

servant of the church which is at Cenchrea. Rom.
16:1. She was commended by the apostle Paul as a
succorer of many and of himself also. Rom. 16:2.
Paul (whom some consider as opposed to women
workers) was assisted by women that worked with
him in the gospel. Phil. 4:3.

Miriam was an anointed prophetess who gave an
exalted message under the inspiration of the Holy
Ghost. Ex. 15:20, 21. Deborah, a recognized
prophetess in Israel (Judges 4:4), was also called
upon to be a "Joan of Arc" to her people. In the
failure of the appointed man to be the leader, she
stepped forward and was blessed of God in performing a man's ministry. This is a fixed precedent, and
justification for those occasional times when it falls
to the lot of women to do the work of men who have
failed. The Bible gives the record of Huldah the
prophetess, to whom Josiah sent to inquire of the
Lord. 2 Kings 22:14. Mary Slessor of Calabar
has won a niche in God's hall of fame for her
dauntless work on the West African coast. The
Pentecostal promise in Joel 2:28, 29, which was
quoted in Acts 2 as partially fulfilled on the day of
Pentecost, has reference to daughters and handmaidens as well as to sons and young men. The present
Pentecostal Movement in further fulfillment of this
beautiful prophecy has brought graphically to light
that God does indeed endow handmaidens and
daughters as well as young men and sons. All these
scriptures and facts clearly and beautifully justify

and confirm them in the exercise of spiritual gifts and ministry.

There is a slight modification, however, in the work and ministry of women, as the Bible indicates. 1 Tim. 2:12; 1 Cor. 11:3. Just as God the Father is greater than the Son, and in the home the man has the final responsiblity, so in the church also positions of administrative leadership are reserved for men. The godly and Scriptural woman (and we think the wise one too) is very happy indeed to leave to her husband or to the men of the church the administrative matters and final decisions in points of government and doctrine. There have been tragedies when women have assumed the leadership of churches which is the prerogative reserved for men. May God give us to allow that full liberty for which the Bible and the Holy Ghost have provided, but to restrain ourselves within these bounds which are clearly prescribed.

Concerning the duty and ministry of the pastor's wife, we would call attention to some of the phases of her ministry in the modern pastorate. She may share his pulpit with him if she is especially endowed with gifts for such a service. She may accompany him in his visits, particularly in cases where there is special need. She can make calls herself in cases where it is not wise or necessary that her husband go. If there is a women's group in the church, she might logically serve as their leader. If she has a particular gift for working with children, how beautiful it would be for her to conduct children's church or serve as a teacher in the Sunday School. If she has administrative ability she might be the Superintendent of the Sunday School or the Principal of the Vacation Bible School. If God has endowed her with musical talent, there may be a place for her in leading the choir and the orchestra, or overseeing the general musical ministry of the church. Many and varied are the ways in which the modern pastor's wife can make herself well-nigh indispensable to the pastor's ministry.

# CHAPTER 6

## The General Character of the Work of the Ministry

"AS every man hath received the gift, even so minister the same one to another, as good stewards of the manifold grace of God." 1 Peter 4:10.

The grace of God is manifold; there are many ways in which it is manifested. As God's grace finds expression through the minister's life, there are many ways in which it reveals itself. How many sides are there to a diamond? Which is the most important? Just as there are innumerable sides to a diamond, and all are equally important, revealing the glory of this lustrous gem, so there are many, many phases of the pastor's life and the manifold grace and glory of our Lord shines forth through them all.

How many names are there for Christ? Which of them is the most accurate? Again we find that the answer is that His names are manifold; and each is correct: each is an accurate one. Alpha, Anointed,

Almighty, Bread of Life, Beginning, Christ, Counsellor, Creator, Door, Everlasting, Eternal, Fairest Among Ten Thousand, First Begotten from the Dead, Good Shepherd, Head of the Church, Immanuel, Jesus, King of kings, Lamb of God, Lily of the Valley, Lord of lords, Mediator, Mighty God, Never-failing Friend, Only Begotten Son, Omega, Omnipotent, Prince of Peace, Preserver, Priest, Prophet, Redeemer, Rose of Sharon, Savior, Son of God, Son of Man, Sustainer, Truth, Unsearchable Riches, Vine, Way, Wonderful Word, More Excellent Way, Your Lord and Mine, and Zealous One. These various names, and many more, portray the Christ in His various capacities and qualities. He is each one of these and infinitely more. It will take eternity to comprehend Him in His fulness.

The church is likewise represented in the Bible by a number of names and figures of speech. She is His body, His bride, the household of faith, the branches, the sheepfold, a great house, an army, a temple, a city, salt, a light, and a kingdom. These are various capacities in which the church is constituted and serves. All are accurate descriptions of her functions and her nature.

In like manner the minister of the gospel is portrayed in the Bible in many ways. The titles given to ministers in God's Word give us a picture of their work and responsibility.

Paul calls Timothy *"a man of God."* 1 Tim. 6:11. What is involved in this solemn title? You

will notice that it is not Timothy who addresses Paul
thus. If it were, we could understand more readily,
for Paul deserves to be called a man of God. Was
not Paul the apostle to the Gentiles? Did he not
found the churches? Was he not the writer of more
New Testament Epistles than any other? These
things would make him worthy of the title "man of
God" indeed. But it is rather his son Timothy, one
of the second generation of gospel preachers, that is
here called a man of God. We understand thus that
this is a title which it is not presumption for us to
take, but which God Himself has intended that we
should have. It implies that we are God's representatives. Men that are full of God, and sent from God.
What a solemn charge! How it must give us dignity
and profound self-consciousness as we go about our
tasks. There is nothing here to inflate us or to be
an occasion of pride; rather, we should be humbly
impressed with the tremendous responsibility that
He has laid upon us. God has certain qualities that
sinners are conscious of—His kindness, love, and
mercy, His justice and impartiality, His condescen-
sion and humility, His holiness and virtue. As men
of God, these Godlike qualities should be found in
us. Would that the world could salute us as men of
God, thus recognizing that we deserve the high title
that the Lord has given us.

"For the priest's lips should keep knowledge, and
they should seek the law at his mouth: for he is the
messenger of the Lord of hosts." Mal. 2:7. Messenger! What is the prerogative of a messenger? Is

it his privilege to tamper with the message that he
has been told to deliver? What of the postman or
the Western Union clerk who opens the mail or who
alters the message received? It is unthinkable that
such liberties should be taken with the communications conveyed from man to man. But what of the
minister of God who makes his own message? "Thus
saith the Lord God, Woe unto the foolish prophets
that follow their own spirit and have seen nothing!"
Ezek. 13:3. It is not the part of the king's messenger to go to the throne room and give the king
about three minutes in which to impart a message
for him to deliver and, if it is not forthcoming in a
stated time, to be up and away, regardless. Men
are tired of listening to each other. There is confusion in the councils of the flesh. The voice of
God is what men want to hear. Our Christ spoke
not as the scribes but with authority. Matt. 7:29.
There is need today for a positive, "Thus saith the
Lord!" and not for the philosophies, theories and
speculations of men. How simple after all is the
duty of the gospel messenger—simply to be a witness
of the things which he has seen and heard. Acts
22:15.

The terms *pastor* (Eph. 4:11) and *shepherd* can
be considered synonymous in many ways. The word
"pastor" is akin to "pasture." It was remarked of
a certain pastor that he was "good pasture." These
words convey to us the rural scene of the quiet
grazing of the sheep and the faithful attendance of
the shepherd. In a number of places in the Word

[ 89 ]

of God His people are referred to as sheep and those who attend them are called shepherds. Psalm 100:3; John 10:1-29; Acts 20:28; 1 Peter 5:2-5. It is the duty of the shepherd to feed, lead, protect, and assist his sheep. He loves them and goes before them. With his rod and his staff he attends them. What a beautiful picture of the tender ministration of a pastor of God's people.

A minister is also called a bishop or *overseer*. 1 Tim. 3:1; Acts 20:28. It is in this capacity particularly that today's pastor is called upon to serve. There are so many counterparts in business life which serve as a pattern or illustration that it is easy to understand. The foreman at the shop, the manager of the plant, or any whose business and responsibility it is to supervise the work of others, must see that each man has his daily task assigned him, that material is provided for him to use, and that his machine is in good working order. When a shortage or breakdown occurs, it is his responsibility to step in and supply the need. He must handle human nature and inspire it to its best accomplishment. He must plan his work for days ahead. He has great responsibility and is often burdened with planning for his work during the hours when his men are at home free from care. No one considers that his work is light. He is recognized as the most capable man in the plant and is given a higher salary. There are so many departments and phases of modern pastoral work that it is the task of the pastor to serve as foreman or supervisor rather than as one who is doing all the work himself. The Lord Jesus at the very beginning of the Christian era spent much of His time in the training of His disciples for the work which they would later perform. The work of the pastor among his various church workers is by way of training them as well as getting work accomplished through them. As Paul exhorted Timothy (2 Tim. 2:2) to commit unto faithful men the words which had been given unto him, that they in turn might be able to teach others also, so it is right and proper that a pastor should have a corps of workers whom he supervises and trains in the work of the gospel.

In Ezek. 3:17 the Lord declares that He had set the prophet as a *watchman* in Israel. He was to warn the wicked of the error of his way and was held responsible if he did not deliver the warning duly. In like manner God has set the present-day pastor as a watchman over his flock and over erring souls round about him. This is not that he is to intrude into personal affairs and pronounce judgment upon people but that he should serve respectfully and seriously as a watcher of the souls of men. It is his responsibility to warn his people of the pitfalls of Satan and also to preach the certainties of God's judgment to a sinning world.

It is also declared in God's Word (2 Cor. 5:20) that ministers particularly are set as *ambassadors* for Christ. This means that we are in a foreign country and have the official position here of representatives of our own native land. Our citizenship is in heaven. We are pilgrims and strangers here. More than that, we are held here with a definite purpose in mind; namely, that we should represent our home government and deliver its messages to the country where we now reside. As with earthly ambassadors, great significance will be attached to our words, for it will be considered that they are the words of the country which we represent. We must therefore guard our speech and control our conduct in that way that will reflect credit to the land that is our own. Here it can be added that at the end of this dispensation just before the declaration of war (the tribulation) between our heavenly country and this wicked world, our own government is going to call its ambassadors home. Praise the Lord! Isa. 26:20.

The minister is likewise considered to be an elder, or *father*. 1 Peter 5:1. This brings to our mind the fact that there must be spiritual maturity on the part of him who serves as pastor of God's people. Not only that, but there should be a providing for his family as an earthly father provides for his. There should be the tender love of the father for his children and the faithful training and educating of his own. As a beloved father in the midst of his family, so a pastor should move among his people.

There are occasions when the pastor is called upon to be a *ruler* of his people. Although he holds this position constantly by virtue of divine ordination (Heb. 13:17), yet it is rarely that his rule is challenged and that it becomes necessary for him to exert his authority. However, it should be continually kept in mind by his people that God has vested him with this responsibility. Although he himself is conscious that God has made him the head over his congregation, yet this should not overly impress him nor should he ever become a lord over God's heritage. 1 Peter 5:3. But it nevertheless remains true that God has endowed him with the right and responsibility of making final decisions in mooted matters and of serving as the appointed director of God's people.

One of the loftiest titles given to men of God is that of *prophet*. Eph. 4:11; Luke 7:26. There comes to mind here a vision of the rugged man of God who appeared before Ahab with the solemn pronouncement, "As the Lord God of Israel liveth, before whom I stand, there shall not be dew nor rain these years but according to my word." 1 Kings 17:1. How daring, and how ominous for the wicked king! He might have considered Elijah as a fanatic who should be retained for observation. But he evidently was conscious of the authority and the power of the unique character that stood before him. John the Baptist likewise hurled his denunciations against Herod, and against the Pharisees and the publicans of his day. This struck terror to their hearts for they knew instinctively that this was the voice of God. Oh, the need in the present hour for men who likewise stand before God and who come forth to deliver God's pronouncements to a wicked age!

A more quiet and routine capacity in which the man of God must serve is that of a *teacher*. 1 Cor. 12:28. It is true that there are certain ones who serve particularly in this role, but it is also true that as the great divine Teacher (Christ Himself and the blessed Holy Ghost) lives within us there must be something of a teaching spirit in every Christian worker. Teaching is the patient, detailed, school-room explanation of the truths of God in that way which is food for the people. This is a very important phase of a minister's work about which we shall say more further on.

A *servant* in the home plays a menial role and is at the beck and call of his employers. A lower social level is his and it is his task to perform that which is assigned him. The Bible clearly depicts the man of God as a servant. 2 Cor. 4:5. We must be humble enough to minister continually to those to whom the Lord has assigned us. This title is a proper balance to that of ruler already observed. It does not contradict it but merely complements it. It is easy to veer to one or the other of these extremes, but we are required to maintain both of these positions at the same time.

There are a number of occupations also that are cited in the Word of God as illustrations of various capacities in which ministers are called to serve: fisherman (Matt. 4:19), guide (Rom. 2:19), nurse (1 Thess. 2:7), builder (1 Cor. 3:10), sower (Matt. 13:3), reaper (John 4:35-38), soldier (2 Tim. 2:3), and laborer. 1 Cor. 3:9.

There are certain qualities in connection with each of these occupations to which attention is called. A

*fisherman* must be patient and also skillful if he is
to succeed in his art. These qualities are needed by
those who would be fishers of men. A *guide* must
know the way, must go before, and must see that
those whom he guides are protected from danger and
advised concerning the path over which they walk.
This is a very good picture of the position of a spiritual guide who goes before and leads his group. A
*nurse* is to attend carefully to the physical needs of
those placed in her charge; or if it is the sick to
whom she ministers she must tenderly and skillfully
respond to every need and carefully nurse the patient
back to health. With little children she must be
true to her charge, being responsible to the mother
at the end of the day. The little children whom the
Lord has committed to our care are not ours, and we
must give account to Him at the end of our day.
Matt. 18:6 warns us of the wrath of our Lord
against those who offend one of the little ones that
believe on Him. How careful then must the minister
be to look after the spiritual interests of those whom
the Lord has committed to his charge.

As *builders* of the house of God we must build
upon the rock Christ Jesus and take heed how we
build. 1 Cor. 3:10. Those who are uncon-
verted must not be built into this building that we
are busy constructing. That day will declare every
man's work of what sort it is. We must therefore
build carefully, cleanly, and according to God's
divine plan; otherwise the great Inspector will con-
demn the work as worthless and there will be nothing

to show for our labor. *Sowing and reaping* are many times divided between workers. One sows and another reaps. John 4:35-38. It requires patience and faith as well as skill to plant the seed and await its harvest. Likewise it is becoming on the part of the reapers to remember that he is only entering into the labors of his predecessor. As a hired harvest hand is subordinate to the farmer who owns the land and sowed the seed in the spring, so the evangelist or succeeding pastor who reaps that which another has sowed is by no means the greater of the two. Let him faithfully reap the golden grain but humbly give the credit to those to whom credit is due.

To be a *soldier* is sometimes a dangerous occupation. It requires courage as well as skill and willingness to submit one's body to the extreme rigors and dangers of warfare. To stand between God and dying men, being responsible for their souls, is to stand in a very solemn place. The great enemy of our souls, through the myriad media which are at his disposal, will attack us relentlessly on every hand. There will be occasions when we will be called upon to endure hardness—physical hardness, and hardness of every other kind. We must not faint in the day of adversity but bravely fight the good fight of faith. "And having vanquished all, stand."

The last title may be considered an anticlimax, but to be a common *laborer* is a respectable thing. The hard, back-breaking work of the laborer represents the diligent toil of the man of God. From early morn till late at night true pastors are carrying the burdens of their people, pouring themselves out in study, prayer, and pastoral visitation, pleading for souls, ministering the Word, and spending long nights of vigil with the ill. It cannot be said of preachers, "They toil not, neither do they spin."

Through the commissions which the Lord gave His disciples and which are also transmitted to us, we likewise can learn something of the nature of the work to which we are called. The titles have to do with the positions which we hold, but the commissions are the instructions which are given to us as we set about our task. The outstanding command which is laid upon Christians of all generations is to preach and to teach the gospel, proclaim and explain, propound and expound. These phases of Christian service will be dealt with at length later, but any consideration of the commissions could not be complete if we did not mention and acknowledge the high importance of these two kinds of ministry.

To the disciples of Matt. 10:16 Jesus said: "I send you forth as sheep in the midst of wolves." We are in one sense shepherds of the sheep committed to our care, yet He tells us that we will be surrounded by dangerous animals as sheep are surrounded by wolves. This is a fair warning of the difficulties which we may expect as we go out into an unfriendly world. He Himself was sent "to preach the gospel to the poor, to heal the brokenhearted, to preach deliverance to the captives and recovering of sight to the blind, to set at liberty them that are bruised, to preach the acceptable year of the Lord." Luke 4:18, 19. And He also says, "As my Father hath sent Me, even so send I you." John 20:21. What a glorious business to be engaged in! What a high and holy calling is ours! He has set us as lights in the world, and has called us the salt of the earth. He has further declared that "he that believeth on Me, the works that I do shall he do also; and greater works than these shall he do; because I go unto My Father." John 14:12. Here is a promise which stands out far ahead of the experience of the average Christian worker. Christ said it, however, and He meant it. May God give us faith to enter into the position of authority and power that He has bequeathed to us in this golden promise.

The great commision begins with the little word "go." Mark 16:15; Matt. 28:19. This is the opposite of sit and dwell, and means forsaking the things that are behind and taking definite action to contact those who are across the road, the city, the county, the state, the nation, and the world. To the uttermost part is His order, beginning at Jerusalem. It is a GO gospel and every spiritual Christian will have a GO in his soul. As we go we are to witness to the things which we have seen and heard.

A more accurate rendering of the word "teach" in Matt. 28:19 is to "make disciples." It is not enough that we shall go merely to discharge our duty and to be clear of the blood of all men. We must not merely pass through and issue our proclamations on the run. But we are told to have as our specific objective the winning of precious souls to Him. We will not have done our duty unless we plead and pray and be patient until men will see the way and walk therein. When Barnabas and Paul came to Iconium they entered into the synagogue of the Jews and "so spake" that a great number believed. Acts 14:1. That is effective speaking. They not only went and witnessed and preached the gospel but they did it in that way that made disciples wherever they went.

# CHAPTER 7

## *Relationships of the Ministry*

L ET us now consider the work of the ministry in its various relationships. This will enable us to get our adjustment and to serve with definite objectives in view. Our chief relationship is to our heavenly Father. The most vital one is to our Lord and Savior Jesus Christ. Our relationship to the church is the most apparent one; that to our official board is the most intimate. And most important is our relationship to the world around us.

In our previous lesson we said that the minister is a servant, but we did not specify whom he serves. Here let it be noted that he is a *servant* in his relationship to God. Matt. 24:45. It is true that he must serve his church as well, but his primary responsibility as a servant is to his Father in heaven. He must receive his instructions from God. His first responsibility is to God. As service to man conflicts with service to God, the latter must be considered the more important. When values are reversed, a man sells his soul and is a timeserver and man-pleaser. This is exceedingly unfortunate and means that he has pulled up anchor and is adrift. The winds and tides of the desires of men will toss him hither and yon and at last dash him to pieces. The minister should get his orders from heaven and carry them through, regardless of all else. To God he gives account at last and so it is God whom he must serve conscientiously day by day.

Now for a most ennobling consideration. God has invited us to *labor with* Him. 1 Cor. 3:9. Some might think, since God finished His work in the six days of Genesis 1 and rested the seventh day, that He is still resting from His labors. But Jesus said in John 5:17, "My Father worketh hitherto and I work." In John 9:4 He declared, "I must work the works of Him that sent Me, while it is day: the night cometh when no man can work." John 4:34 states, "My meat is to do the will of Him that sent Me, and to finish His work." So Christ during His lifetime was a co-laborer with God. And now that high privilege is bestowed upon us. What is the task at which God and we are laboring? The first creation was completed in six days. He is now engaged in bringing into existence that mystical yet marvelous new creation. 2 Cor. 5:17; Gal. 6:15; Eph. 4:24; Col. 3:10. This is an intricate and important work and how honored are we to be called to engage in it with Him. In the yoke with us (Matt. 11:30) is none other than our wonderful heavenly Father. If we lie down or lag behind we delay and hinder Him. God grant unto us to do our part in this great labor and ministry.

Paul said, "Let a man so account of us as of the ministers of Christ and *stewards* of the mysteries of God." 1 Cor. 4:1. A steward is one who has been placed in charge of another man's goods. The goods that have been committed to our care are the marvelous mysteries of the kingdom. "To whom God would make known what is the riches of the glory of this mystery among the Gentiles: which is Christ in you, the hope of glory." Col. 1:27. "And without controversy, great is the mystery of godliness." 1 Tim. 3:16. "Behold, I show you a mystery; we shall not all sleep, but we shall all be changed." 1 Cor. 15:51. "But in the days of the voice of the seventh angel, when he shall begin to sound, the mystery of God should be finished, as He hath declared to His servants the prophets." Rev. 10:7. These mysteries are to be understood by us in the first place. They are the mysteries which belong unto God and His kingdom. We are instructed by our Lord not to keep secret these mysteries but rather to proclaim them abroad. Paul said in Eph. 3:8, 9, "Unto me . . . is this grace given, to *make all men see* what is the fellowship of the mystery." Not just simply to proclaim it, and inform them that there is a mystery, or tantalize them with a partial knowledge of it. It is our duty to do our very utmost to explain these mysteries to the sons of men, and actually to make them see and understand. God has given us this task and we are responsible to Him for its performance.

There is a difference between a *trustee* and a steward. A steward's relationship to the owner is that of employee to employer; whereas a trustee's relationship to the owner who has bestowed the trust upon him is to one who has died or who stands in the background. It is a matter which is safeguarded by provisions and penalties of the law. To serve as a trustee of funds places one under certain legal responsibilities which must be discharged under penalty of fine or imprisonment or both. It is a serious business to act as a trustee. Now God has put us in trust with the gospel. 1 Thess. 2:4. As the courier carries the message of pardon for the condemned criminal from the governor to the warden, and must deliver it on time lest the man die needlessly, so we have been entrusted with the message of pardon for those who will die if we do not deliver it. It is a serious business to be put in trust with the gospel.

The Word also declares that God has placed us in the position of *priest* before Him and on behalf of the people. 1 Peter 2:9. As Abraham interceded on behalf of Lot and was heard to the saving of that man and his wife and daughters, and as Moses interceded on behalf of the whole nation of Israel and was heard and responded to, so God has given us the privilege of standing before Him to intercede on behalf of dying men here below. How little do we enter into this privilege, and how seldom do we stand in this most powerful position of intercessor between the living and the dead. But it is our privilege, and it may be that there is real guilt resting upon us if we fail to serve our God and a lost world in this capacity.

This question of guilt becomes more serious still when we look at Ezek. 3:17, 18. "Son of man, I have made thee a *watchman* unto the house of Israel: therefore hear the word at My mouth, and give them warning from Me. When I say unto the wicked, Thou shalt surely die; and thou givest him not warning, nor speakest to warn the wicked from his wicked way, to save his life; the same wicked man shall die in his iniquity; but his blood will I require at thy hand." What is the meaning of this last phrase, "His blood will I require at thy hand? There are wicked people all about us who continue in sin day after day. God in His mercy does not cut them off, "not willing that any should perish." He gives them further and further opportunity to repent and turn to Him. They will never repent until they are warned of their sin. The warning must come in stringent tones and with the authority of the Lord Jehovah. He has instructed us to give this warning. If we give it not, the blood of the wicked will He require at our hand. When He required Abel's blood at the hand of Cain He banished him from His presence and made him a fugitive and a vagabond on the earth. In the Noahic covenant He declared, in Genesis 9:6, "Whoso sheddeth man's blood, by man shall his blood be shed." Ezekiel 3:19 declares that if we warn a man we have delivered our souls. Does this imply that if we warn him not our souls are in jeopardy and the blood of the lost will be required of us? This is too solemn a question to answer. However, it is surely serious enough to give us grave concern lest we be negligent of our duty of serving as God's watchman for men.

To our Lord Jesus we serve as His *undershepherds*. 1 Peter 5:2-4; Acts 20:28. He is the Chief Shepherd. This implies that there are many under Him, and there surely are. He has told us to feed His sheep and to take heed unto their welfare. This constitutes us as shepherds and we serve under Him whose sheep they are. As David referred to "my father's sheep," so we must realize that the sheep whom we shepherd belong to the Chief Shepherd and not us. This will prevent our becoming lords over God's heritage; using them to our material, personal advantage on the one hand, or assuming too great a burden of responsibility on the other hand. We must serve our Chief Shepherd well, carrying out His instructions day by day, doing as He would have us do and as He Himself would do under all circumstances. But if conditions get out of our control and situations arise over which we are powerless, we can cast our burden upon the Lord and remember after all that they are His sheep and not ours. If He can afford to let these conditions exist, then it is His responsibility and not ours. Go to bed, and sleep the sleep of the just, and leave the results with Him.

Quite a contrast to this thought is that expressed in 2 Cor. 11:2 and Rev. 19:7-9. While we serve our Lord as undershepherds here, there is a love relationship between us which is going to culminate one day at the marriage supper of the lamb. As a wife works for her husband and is happy to do so, and at the same time sustains such an entirely different and more precious relationship to him compared with others, so we, as we work for our Master day by day, are also conscious of the fact that we are His own *betrothed*, the object of His heart's affections, and we lavish on Him our love and our labor of love. This gracious and most satisfying relationship sustains and upgirds us through the weary hours of our labor here. We are His, and He is ours, and some day the world will know that He is our Bridegroom and we are His bride.

Our relationship to the church over which God has assigned us is one which is real and apparent. They know and the world knows that we are their pastor. But the phases of our relationship to them are not as apparent to the world as they are to us. For one thing, we are *watchers* for their souls. Heb. 13:17. There are so many things which need to be watched over in connection with our people that this phase of our ministry to them is very important. The spirituality of the entire assembly as they worship together, and that of each individual in the congregation, must be our concern. Wolves must be warned against and warded off if possible. Those who stumble must be picked up and those who wander away must be brought home. Ezek. 34:4. As a sentinel in the night, and a herder of the sheep by day, we pace up and down and watch over our people with jealous care.

As with every large family and group of human beings, there will always arise questions of discipline and problems of human nature. If there were no order, government, and authority in our churches, they would soon become places of turmoil. They would eventually disintegrate were it not given unto one to exercise genuine authority and to be recognized as the *ruler* and head. God has ordained that the pastor should serve in this capacity. By the ruling of his own immediate family he demonstrates whether or not he will be able to serve his church as ruler. 1 Tim. 3:4, 5. He is not qualified to serve a church as pastor if he is unable to bring up his own children in the nurture and admonition of the Lord and command respect and obedience in his own household.

To be a ruler and leader of the people implies seniority of experience and ability. A man is definitely unable to instruct and direct others unless he himself is able to perform as a pattern and example. Human nature covets a position of rulership and authority. To hold the place of a leader in an assembly may seem to be desirable and gratifying to the flesh. But let such a one remember that his position of leadership involves also the obligation to be more mature, more spiritual, more faithful, more prayerful, and more godly than any of his members. A leader must be out in front in accomplishment as well as in authority. Let every pastor take diligent care that he is an *example* to the flock in everything. Paul actually invited his people to follow him as he followed Christ. Phil. 3:17; 1 Tim. 1:16.

The purpose of being placed in the position of ruler over His household is that we might *give them meat* in due season. As every home and army and group of people must have physical food for sustenance, so the group whom the Lord has placed in our care as spiritual beings and new creatures in Christ must be given spiritual food for their daily sustenance. Such matters are utterly unknown to those who are not born again. But it is the pastor's business not only to know what spiritual food is, but to be able to prepare and serve it in an acceptable manner. He must be faithful in nourishing the new converts and older saints alike with that spiritual food which all must have. This is a MUST, as preparing meals is a *must* to a mother. Other ministries fit in around it but when the time comes this must be done and done well. Without it all other ministry is in vain, as without food our bodies perish. Carelessness and inefficiency along this line will result in dissatisfaction, malnutrition, non-resistance to spiritual disease, and eventual discharge as a servant who was appointed to feed his people.

The inside circle of the church fellowship is the group known as the official board. To this the pastor is most vitally related. As the wife lives so close to her husband that unless there is love between them friction is bound to result, so the relation between the pastor and his board must be cemented by love or else there will be difficulty. Right here we have the test of the pastor's character in which many men have failed. With a disgusted gesture, some would sweep the deck clear of all official boards and govern the church alone. But if we cannot bow and yield and rule our own spirits, how are we qualified to minister to others who day by day are called upon to humble themselves and serve those around them?

It might be stated in one sentence that the relation of the pastor to his official board is that of an elder brother, and chairman, and senior member of a counselling committee. There must be a comradeship between him and them in the sense that is not shared with the other members of the church. There are matters which they hold in confidence among themselves which should not be divulged to others. He should inspire their love as well as their confidence and be a real leader among them.

Neither should the pastor forget that he and his people are instructed by the Redeemer of men to complete the redemption of the world by persuading men to accept salvation. The church is not complete and the Lord cannot rest until it is. He still is seeking to save that which is lost. They who are filled with the Spirit will do likewise.

To the world round about, the pastor and his

people serve as *lights* in a dark place. Phil. 2:15.
They are to be examples of the marvelous saving
grace of the Master. They are to demonstrate His
great transforming power. They are to be a constant proof and reproof to the world concerning the
things of the Kingdom.

The apostle Paul declared himself in one sense to
be a *savior* of men. "To the weak became I as weak,
that I might gain the weak: I am made all things
to all men, that I might by all means save some."
1 Cor. 9:22. It is not sufficient that we stand as a
fixed lighthouse with its constant service to mariners,
but we should man the lifeboats, take the initative,
and do our best to save some. With all the pastor's
busy-ness in looking after members of his own flock,
he should not forget that there are hundreds round
about him who may be dependent upon him for their
very salvation.

This zeal for the salvation of souls which should
be manifested in his very spirit and personal conduct
and contact with men will crystallize itself into sermons which are directed to the lost. As Paul exhorted Timothy to do the work of an *evangelist* (2 Tim.
4:5), so it is very proper that the pastor should
devote, say, the Sunday evening service to an evangelistic appeal. By this means he makes a personal
effort, leads his people likewise to make personal
effort, and has made it public knowledge that his
church is concerned for the salvation of men.

In concluding this chapter upon the relationships

of the ministry it might be well to add some comments concerning the inter-relation of the pastor and his church. As the heavenly Father and His eternal Son are one in essence and substance, love each other with an everlasting love, and the Son respects the Father as greater than He; and as the husband and wife are one in flesh as well as in spirit, name, and objective in life, and the wife respects the husband as the head of the home; in like manner, the pastor and his church stand together. They are to be one in spirit and objective, in name, in love, and in reality. It is true that he is the head and they the body, but there never need be even a reminder of the subordination of the one to the other. The Scriptures themselves declare this relationship. The pastor should serve his people. 2 Cor. 4:5. He should love them dearly. 1 Thess. 2:8; Phil. 1:7. He should also give himself unstintingly on their behalf. 2 Cor. 12:15. They in turn should gladly serve him. 2 Cor. 8:5. They should love him respectfully (1 Thess. 5:13), and give generously to his support and well-being. 1 Cor. 9:11; Gal. 6:6.

# CHAPTER 8

## The Minister and His Ministry

THERE are certain distinct tasks and objectives which a minister should have in his ministry. Foremost of these is the *preaching* of the Word. The Lord has ordained that by the foolishness of preaching men should be saved. 1 Cor. 1:21. He manifests His Word through preaching. Titus 1:3. Paul preached from Jerusalem and round about unto Illyricum (Rom. 15:19), and was delivered from Nero that by him the preaching might be fully known. 2 Tim. 4:17. There is tremendous power in the Word of God as it is conveyed to the hearers by preaching. This Word effects conversion in the first place. James 1:21; 1 Peter 1:23. It enables new-born babes to grow. 1 Peter 2:2. It has sanctifying power. John 17:17. By it we are kept from sin. Psalm 119:11. It reveals the hidden things of the heart (Heb. 4:12), and accomplishes the purpose whereunto the Lord has sent it. Isa. 55:11. It gives us faith to believe for the answer to our prayer (John 15:17), and it constitutes that standard by which we shall be judged at the last day. John 12:48. It is no wonder then that we are instructed to "preach the Word." 2 Tim. 4:2. Let us beware—that we do not preach ourselves (2 Cor. 4:5), our education, our experience, our achievements, or anything that reflects credit to us. Let us incessantly and forever preach Christ Jesus our Lord and the wonderful Word He has given us.

As a companion and counterpart to the preaching of the gospel there must be the *teaching* of the Word of God. When Jesus was on earth He was called a Teacher more often than anything else. When He ministered to people, pouring forth words of love and wisdom, it is recorded that He went about all the cities and villages teaching in their synagogues and preaching the gospel of the kingdom. Matt. 9:35. When He left His great commission to the disciples it included the injunction to teach (Matt. 28:19, 20), as well as the command to preach the gospel. Mark 16:15. This two-fold ministry was faithfully performed by the early disciples, for "they ceased not to teach and preach Jesus Christ." Acts 5:42. Paul's ministry consisted of preaching and teaching (Col. 1:28), and the last view which the New Testament gives of him shows him in his own hired house in Rome preaching the kingdom of God and teaching those things which concern the Lord Jesus Christ. Acts 28:31.

[ 113 ]

As a permanent institution in the Christian church, the Lord has set and established the office of a teacher. 1 Cor. 12: 28. Likewise the gift of teaching is listed among the gifts of the Holy Ghost which are imparted to His church, and which belong to that church for her use and keeping. Rom. 12:7. "When He ascended up on high he led captivity captive and gave gifts unto men. He gave some, apostles; and some, prophets; and some, evangelists; and some, pastors and teachers." Eph. 4:8, 11. Notice four classes here: apostles, prophets, evangelists, and pastors-and-teachers. This last class refers to one individual with two functions to his ministry. He should be a shepherd of the sheep and a feeder as well. This gives us the picture of what Christ was and what He commanded us to be; of what the early disciples and Paul were and what we present-day disciples should be. It explains to us that it is the will of God that the *teaching* ministry of the church should be just as strong as that of preaching.

It may be said that by preaching men are brought into the kingdom and by teaching they are held and confirmed. The birth of a baby is a marvel and a miracle. A new creature is brought into being. But this is the beginning rather than the end, and the baby must be nourished and sustained lest the little life disappear, and the miracle be lost. How great then is the importance of the day-by-day teaching of the Word of God to new-born babes that they may grow thereby. If each church were as careful to preserve its converts by the refined art of skillful and faithful teaching as it is zealous to bring them into the Kingdom, then there would not be so many backsliders to block the way to heaven and themselves be gospel-hardened and eventually lost. Let leaders of the churches take particular note; let them carefully obey the instructions of our Lord, and present a balanced gospel of preaching and teaching His Wonderful Word.

As this stream of divine truth flows forth to the people, it is the pastor's responsibility to keep a careful watch on the services of his church. They must be kept spiritual. It is a mark of apostasy and utterly displeasing to the Lord if our services have a form of godliness and are devoid of His power. Form is essential to beauty and order, but a lifeless form is a corpse. There must be vitality, vibrancy, and spiritual reality in our worship. They that worship the Father must worship Him in spirit and in truth, for the Father seeketh such to worship Him. John 4:23, 24. Where the Spirit of the Lord is there is liberty. 2 Cor. 3:17. God wills that there shall be sweet personal liberty and sincere spontaneous expression in our worship of Him.

But on the other hand it is displeasing to the Lord and altogether unedifying if "the whole church be come together in one place and all speak with tongues," for instance. There are other extravagances as well, and they equally cause our listeners to say that we are mad. 1 Cor. 14:23. There is a distinct

Scriptural regulation for the operation of the gifts of the Spirit and those who conform to these regulations will find that there is not only power in these gifts but beauty and edification as well. The spirits of the prophets are subject to the prophets (1 Cor. 14:32), and there is no need for extravagance and fanaticism in Holy Ghost worship. A divine balance should be struck between these two extremes. Our services should be altogether spiritual and Pentecostal (Eph. 5:18), and neither formal nor fanatical.

We believe that it is the will of God that all Christians should receive the Baptism in the Holy Ghost. Acts 2:38, 39. As the apostles which were at Jerusalem were not content to allow the church at Samaria to remain long without the Holy Ghost baptism, sending down to them Peter and John that they might receive the Holy Ghost, so it is not the will of God today that Christians should remain long without the same Pentecostal baptism. Where a church does not have those who receive the baptism of the Holy Spirit, it is evident that there is something of a declension or lack of Holy Ghost power. Where individuals do receive the baptism of the Holy Spirit as on the day of Pentecost, it can be taken as good evidence of life and faith and the power of God in the services.

Faithfulness to the Word of God also requires us to reiterate the teaching of the apostle Paul, "Quench not the Spirit; despise not prophesying; desire spiritual gifts, but rather that ye may prophesy; and forbid

not to speak with tongues." 1 Thess. 5:19, 20;
1 Cor .14:1, 39. The gifts of the Spirit are God's
gracious enduement from heaven and are not to be
despised or rejected. They were placed in the church
as manifestations and divinely appointed expressions
of the Holy Spirit in His work in this dispensation.
Why should we let the Philistines fill up these wells
of our fathers and stop their flow of power and
blessing? Let us dig them again and witness once
more the manifestation of the supernatural and the
miraculous which characterized the Gospel teaching
of the first century.

Another task which falls to the lot of the pastor
is to *maintain his church in peace and love and unity.*
A favorite tactic of the devil is to break the unity of
the Spirit and bring envy and strife; and where this
is, there is confusion and every evil work. James
3:16. It is the pastor's responsibility to keep close
contact with his people and do his best to smother
out incipient flames of dissension and strife. A little
fire is more easily extinguished than a large one. How
wise is the pastor who brings all effort to bear to ex-
tinguish the little blaze ere it consume his entire house
and himself. Unity prevailed on the day of Pentecost and was vital to blessing. The outstanding
prayer of the Master for His disciples was that they
should love one another. John 13:34. Love is the
first fruit of the Spirit and that more excellent way
without which all gifts are in vain. Gal. 5:22;

[ 117 ]

1 Cor. 12:31; 1 Cor. 13:2. This responsibility may well be considered among the most important of those that rest upon the pastor.

It is stated that the work of the pastor is to *perfect the saints.* Eph. 4:13. This was Paul's objective, as he declared in Col. 1:28, striving mightily to present every man perfect in Christ Jesus. It should be apparent that birth into the kingdom and reception into the church do not constitute and consummate the perfection of the saints. The process is then only begun. From spiritual birth on "until we come in the unity of the faith and of the knowledge of the Son of God unto a perfect man, unto the measure of the stature of the fulness of Christ," it is the pastor's part to feed and lead, to stimulate and inspire, and do all that he can toward perfecting the saints.

Incident to this perfecting of the saints, and necessary to it, there is the problem of *keeping our individual members from slipping* away. Elders are enjoined to take heed unto themselves and to all the flock over which the Holy Ghost hath made them overseers. Acts 20:28. When Jesus came to the end of His earthly ministry He was able to report to His Father, "Those that Thou gavest Me I have kept, and none of them is lost but the son of perdition, that the Scripture might be fulfilled." John 17:12. May God give His present-day shepherds the same faithful, diligent care for the sheep that they too may be able to report at the end of their day that they have kept those that were committed unto them.

It is the pastor's responsibility to keep a watchful
eye for latent or incipient talent among the members
of his church. It is his task to stimulate and *give
exercise and training* to those individuals who manifest gifts of the Spirit or evidence of being called into
Christian ministry. Every talent should be invested
for the Lord (Matt. 25:14, 30) and all gifts of the
Spirit should be given opportunity for development
and use. Heb. 5:14. Many Sunday School teachers
will be needed. It will be helpful to have assistance
in the preliminary part of the worship service. There
will be auxiliary meetings and services for the different
age levels and of various groups and agencies of the
church, all of which will need leaders and other
participants. It will be his task to discover those
who are capable of serving in these various capacities
and to use them to perform these ministries. The
Lord Jesus Christ spent much of His time in training
the twelve apostles. He took them with Him where-
ever He went. He gave them valuable teaching. He
also sent them out on trial journeys to exercise their
budding gifts and develop their coming powers. This
strategy was most successful, for at His death His
disciples were trained and equipped and able to carry
on the ministry of their Master. The apostle Paul
followed the same divine pattern. There were at
least eighteen individuals who are mentioned by
name as those who at one time or another traveled
with him and learned his ways. 1 Cor. 4:17. To
one of these, Timothy by name, he sent this instruc-

tion, "The things that thou has heard of me among many witnesses, the same commit thou to faithful men who shall be able to teach others also." 2 Tim. 2:2. This is important instruction to present-day Timothys as well.

The pastor must infuse into his people *an evangelistic spirit and vision*. As Christ taught His disciples to lift up their eyes and look upon the harvest field, so it is His will that His under-shepherds should teach their people to do likewise. He has told us to go out into the highways and hedges and compel them to come in. He still is "come to seek and to save that which is lost." This objective can be gained by the example of the pastor in his own personal life and by devoting at least one service a week to making an evangelistic appeal. He must inspire and lead his people in crusades and campaigns for the salvation of the lost and the upbuilding of the kingdom.

This vision and passion for the salvation of souls should not be limited to the neighborhood or the city in which the church is located. The apostolic command is that we go into all the world and preach the gospel to every creature. It is the will of God that strong effort be made for *the evangelization of the world*. It cannot be other than true that God is depending upon the Christians of each generation to evangelize that entire generation. No others can do it. They must arise and follow the Master in their vision, in their prayer, in their gifts, and in their personal consecration, to the very ends of the earth. A missionary church is a God-blessed church; and the unselfishness of the poured-out life on behalf of those whom they have not seen in the flesh, as exemplified by the apostle Paul (Col. 2:1), is the true spirit of Christ. It is the very genius of Christianity, and that devotion and true spirit of God with which He is well pleased. John 12:25, 26.


When Jesus went about preaching the gospel of the kingdom and teaching in their synagogues, He also was *healing* every sickness and every disease among the people. Matt. 9:35. He has promised that "these signs shall follow them that believe: . . . they shall lay hands on the sick and they shall recover." Mark 16:17, 18. A definite part of the atonement which He wrought upon the cross is that we should be healed in our bodies as well as saved in our souls. Isa. 53:5. This doctrinal and experiential emphasis the Holy Ghost has given to the church in these last days. We cannot afford to lose it as the church in the Middle Ages did. Truly the power of God is just the same today and there is as great a need for the miraculous to confirm His preached Word as there ever was. We must not only teach the Bible doctrine of divine healing but we must encourage our people by our precedent and precept to live up to their full opportunities in this regard. A divine healing service held often in our regular church schedule, and sermons on this theme from time to time, will provide a practical means for continued interest in this important part of gospel ministry.

The Lord was not satisfied that Moses or Joshua should be content with settling down short of the full possession of the promised land. "Ye have compassed this mountain long enough." Deut. 2:3. "Speak unto the children of Israel that they go forward." Ex. 14:15. Our Master set His face stedfastly toward Jerusalem, and the apostle Paul had his vision set on Rome and Spain and as far as his ministry would take him. It is not the spirit of Christ or the gospel to be satisfied with that measure of accomplishment to which we have already attained. There is yet much land to be possessed. There are souls to be saved and areas to be occupied for God. Self-complacency is of the devil, and the church that is satisfied with its accomplishment and that settles down merely to maintain the status quo has begun the backward march and the process of deterioration. The pastor must be *a man of vision*. He must look upon the fields round about and sense that they are ripe for the harvest and awaiting his sickle. He must inspire his church with a desire for accomplishment for God and the salvation of lost souls. With God all things are possible, and He has told us to ask that our joy may be full. We have not because we ask not. It is the will of God that we move on with Him. William Carey's challenge, "Attempt

great things for God; expect great things from God,"
rings in our ears today and beckons us onward.

There is a difference between having vision and
being visionary. In the mental sketch of the conquest ahead spiritual imagination should be properly
balanced with *good common sense.* From a church
capacity of one hundred and a small group of saints
in a small town it would hardly be wise or within the
realm of rational faith to plan for an auditorium
seating five thousand. First attempt that which is
easily within the realm of possibility, and then launch
forward to greater undertaking. Your plan will
appear more likely to be a leading of the Lord and
His plan for your church if you take one step at a
time in a forward move. As God Himself has given
you the vision and the faith for its realization He
will inspire others to stand with you and to follow
when the time arrives.

Right here there sometimes comes a break and a
breach which leads to the ruin of the ambitious pastor.
If his faith, his vision, and his spirit of leadership
are not tempered with *patience and forbearance* toward the slower-moving members of his official board
and congregation, he may plunge on to the disruption
of the fellowship and unity of his local church and
thus effect a division of that church rather than lead
it on to the greater accomplishment which he had
in mind. This is disastrous—a trick of the enemy.
If the plan is of God, proper confirmation will come
in due time, and it is a wholesome chastening of one's

own spirit and an exercise of genuine faith to be willing to wait for God Himself to bring unanimity of purpose, faith, and desire among the people. With a God-given vision before him he should lead firmly but gently on to that end.

The various elements of the pastor's ministry which have been cited in this chapter will contribute toward the church's growth. It cannot be otherwise. These things are as food, water, air, and physical exercise to the growing child. As the church organism has life within it and more particularly the life of God, *it will grow* and develop as these phases of the pastor's ministry are attended to. It is the will of God that His house shall be filled (Luke 14:23), and that the church of God shall develop "unto a perfect man, the measure of the stature of the fulness of Christ." Eph. 4:15; 2 Peter 1:8; 3:18.

A final word of exhortation may be in order. The main elements of a pastor's ministry are outlined above and with them there are two general considerations to keep in mind. First we must be conscious of our own inability and our entire insufficiency. "We are not sufficient of ourselves, to think anything as of ourselves." 2 Cor. 3:5. "Without Me ye can do nothing." John 15:5. This lesson we learn first of all, and also have it continually borne in upon us as we live and work for Him. But over against it there comes this blessed assurance, "Our sufficiency is of God." 2 Cor. 3:5. Has He not said, "My grace is sufficient for thee"? 2 Cor. 12:9. Faith in this fact inspired the apostle Paul to say, "I can do all things through Christ which strengtheneth me." Phil. 4:13. We are more than conquerors through Him that loved us. Rom. 8:27.

# CHAPTER 9

## *Church Organization*

C HURCH organization is figuratively presented in Paul's description of the body of Christ. "From whom the whole body, fitly joined together and compacted by that which every joint supplieth, according to the effectual working in the measure of every part, maketh increase of the body unto the edifying of itself in love." Eph. 4:16; 2:21. It is simply the integration of joint and part into one united whole so that together all can function as one unit efficiently and harmoniously.

The purpose of church organization is threefold. In the first place its purpose is to conform to the nature of God. The Lord Himself is orderly. His great celestial universe moves with that precision which makes it possible for astronomers to foretell the exact time of eclipses, the appearance of comets, and other celestial phenomena. He instructed the children of Israel to move according to specific rank and precedence and directed the exact position in the camp of each tribe in relation to the Tabernacle in the center. When Christ fed the five thousand He commanded them to be seated by companies, in ranks by hundreds and by fifties. Mark 6:39, 40. The human body, itself His own handiwork, is a marvel of exquisite precision and organization. The timing of the heart action and the breathing of the lungs, the digestive processes and the relation of the nervous system to all parts of the body, are in perfect order and co-operation. They all function automatically and involuntarily, set by the hand of the skilled Maker of a marvelous mechanism. Can anyone doubt that He would be pleased to have the body of His own Son organized and inter-related with the most careful precision? Certainly it is in perfect harmony with the plan and methods of God in His great world that His church, His choicest creation, should have at least as great a degree of harmony and unity in its functioning as any other of His works.

In the second place, the purpose of church organization is to provide a maximum of efficiency. A mob of ten thousand could be routed by a company of one hundred soldiers through the orderliness and compactness of their action. In like manner a church that is knit together with everyone assigned to his place (Mark 3:34), can accomplish much more for God than a large, unorganized mass of Christians who happen to worship under the same roof. There is much work to be done in this big needy world. It is common sense and intelligence to prepare for the accomplishment of that work in the most efficient manner possible.

In the third place, the purpose of church organization is to insure fairness in its administration. A small group who constitute a closed corporation could monopolize the ownership and legal privileges if the church were not fully organized. There could easily be partiality in the amount of ministry given the various members in the church's activity and a preponderence of attention given to a few if there were no records or system.

In contemplating the organizing of a church, it is presupposed and assumed that there is first of all a group of thoroughly born-again souls on hand. This is the only material from which a true church can be built. Is it not said that there is no other foundation than that which is laid, even Jesus Christ? 1 Cor. 3:11. The church is a company of people who have been born again and who belong to His spiritual kingdom. John 3:3; Matt. 18:3. Any other than born-again souls builded into the church of God are only wood, hay, and stubble, to be consumed by the fire of that day. 1 Cor. 3:12, 13. How foolish is the pastor who spends his time building such material into God's holy temple.

With the material of born-again people on hand, the pastor sets about the construction of the church organization. Just to assemble at stated times for public worship, allowing whosoever will to come,

and continuing thus, is not building a church. There
must be the act of organizing, or setting in order. The
first step toward organizing a church is to determine
and recognize a definite membership. There are
reasons why there should be a definite church membership. First, it supplies the need which is instinctive
in every Christian's heart for a church home. Just
as human hearts desire to have a place called home
and desire to live there as much as possible, so it is
instinctive for new creatures in Christ to desire a
church home. There is an element of permanence
about an organized work which naturally appeals
to people. They do not want to run the risk of association with something that is temporary or tran-
sient. In order to meet this need and have a place
where people can settle down and be at home, giving
them a sense of "belonging," it is necessary to effect
an organization with a definite membership.

Another reason why there should be a definite
church membership is that it is Scriptural. In the
days of the apostles and of the early church, it is
recorded "of the rest durst no man join himself to
them, but the people magnified them, and believers
were the more added to the Lord, multitudes both of
men and women." Acts 5:13-14. This reveals a
very definite membership and a distinct line of demarkation between the early disciples and the people
of the world. That is the way it should be, and a
definite membership is necessary to effect a distinct
line of demarkation. It is clearly seen in a number of
scriptures by the actual numbers of early church

membership given, that a count was made and a record kept. There were 120 on the day of Pentecost. Acts 1:15. Three thousand were added to the church that day. Acts 2:21. Later the number of men was increased to five thousand. Acts 4:4.

The instructions concerning discipline make it clear that there was a distinct line on one side of which the members were, and on the other side of which they were to be placed if they no longer deserved fellowship. 1 Cor. 5:2, 13. The apostle Paul said that the church at Corinth should put away that wicked person from among themselves. Here is an "in" and an "out" which is possible only when there is a definite membership. The Lord Himself instructed that, after proper preliminary steps toward reconciliation, an irreconcilable brother was to be counted as a heathen and a publican. Matt. 18:17. This put him outside the pale of the Christian community and required that he begin all over again if he desired Christian fellowship. This requirement also reveals His expectation that there should be an "in" and "out" of church membership. Titus 3:10 calls for the rejection of a heretic after the first or second admonition. How could there be a rejection if there were not a group from which he could be expelled? See also 2 Thess. 3:6, 14, 15.

There is still another reason why it is proper that there should be a definite church membership. It is wise and fair from a business standpoint. When individuals attend a church and invest in it as their

church home they have a financial interest in it. If
it is owned by an individual (the pastor, for instance) and he later sells the property and moves to
another city, then those who have worshiped there
feel that their church roof has been sold over their
heads and a grave injustice has been done them. Who
can deny that there is justice in their feeling? To
give such individuals a vote concerning the disposal of
their home seems to be elementary right and justice.
Again, if anyone is allowed to vote who happens to
be present at a business meeting, this would give
strangers and those who attend very infrequently
just as much voice in the control of the church property as those who had been faithful in attendance
and who had real investment therein. This would be
injustice and occasion for legitimate protest. Both of
these possibilities are avoided by the simple expedient
of having a definite membership roll and the ownership of the property vested in that membership. This
is not only sensible and eminently fair but there are
Scripture passages which confirm this principle. Rom.
12:17 tells us to provide things honest in the sight
of all men. 2 Cor. 8:21 enjoins us, "Providing for
honest things, not only in the sight of the Lord, but
also in the sight of men."

Before a definite church membership can be determined and recognized, the question of a standard of
membership should first be settled. It is not best to
let the pastor or even the official board use their
personal judgment in the matter of acceptance or rejection into membership or expelling from member-

ship. There should be a written pattern or straight-edge by which impartial decisions may be made. Rule by law and not by person is the accepted thing in our democracy, and why should it not likewise be in our churches? To have a definite black and white understanding as to the qualifications for membership makes for confidence and satisfaction among the people. Just to have it "generally understood" will result in its being often misunderstood. There is nothing like having a definite document which is always neutral and not influenced by argument, which can quietly render a verdict on each mooted question. Have a clear understanding of what is involved and have it written down in simple, concise English and adopted by the voluntary vote of the church membership if there is such, or by responsible church officials in the case of a new church. This will put an end to argument and make for peaceful administration of church affairs.

A definite born-again experience is necessary for membership in the church. 2 Cor. 5:17. But should we be content with a mere verbal confession of faith, and a recitation of the sentence: "I believe in Jesus Christ as the Son of God"? There have been many groups around us who have associated themselves together on such a basis. By all appearances, there are many goats in such flocks. There should be something more specific in the way of requirement for church membership. The Lord has commanded, "Come out from among them, and be ye separate." 2 Cor. 6:17. He has also instructed us, "Be ye holy, for I am holy." 1 Peter 1:16. He has told us that "if any man love the world, the love of the Father is not in him." 1 John 2:15. Likewise, "Let no man deceive you with vain words: for because of these things" (certain sins just enumerated) "cometh the wrath of God upon the children of disobedience." Eph. 5:6. What are we to do in the face of these scriptures? Shall we take into our church membership those in whom there is very evidently a love for the world? If the wrath of God is resting upon certain individuals, and they shall in no wise enter into the kingdom (Gal. 5:19-21), what right have we and how wise are we to accept them into the church? There should be a definite statement concerning renunciation of sin and the things of the world, and a clear understanding on this point.

If we claim that our church is right, and that we have received an experience and believe doctrines that are distinctive and Scriptural, then consistency requires that we expect of our church members a high standard of spiritual life and experience. If our church is no different from other churches, then why do we exist as a separate denomination? This is a distinct challenge. Christianity is already split into too many denominations and sects. Unless there is a clear justification for our separate existence as a denomination, then we stand condemned for having increased the number. Our very existence as a church demands that we have a distinct and higher standard of membership, and certain qualifications for membership not to be found in other communions.

If we have a clean church and a holy church, it will react favorably before God and man. Sin crucified our Master. This vile world is an enemy of grace. The church is en route to a holy heavenly home and we worship a holy God. This requires that our membership be as nearly as possible without spot or wrinkle or any such thing, but holy and without blemish, a glorious church. Eph. 5:27. God is far more likely to pour His blessings upon a clean communion of saints than upon those who harbor sin and worldliness in their midst. The world likewise will appreciate the consistency in clean living of those who make strong profession. Thus their mouths will be stopped and their hearts convinced that there is reality and power in this wonderful salvation.

After a clean, high standard of membership has been erected and individuals accepted on that basis and a church membership thus constituted, the next order of business is the election of deacons. The first deacons were chosen by the believers, as recorded in Acts 6:1-7. The Bible standard for the choice of deacons has been given us by the apostle Paul in 1 Tim. 3:8-13. There were deacons in the church at Philippi as is revealed by the apostle Paul in Phil. 1:1. An entire chapter will later be devoted to the qualifications and duties of the deacons of the church.

Suffice it now to call attention to the fact that in the organization of a church there should be a properly constituted deacon board.

What is a church without a Sunday School? As there are sufficient young people to constitute a distinct band, then let them be organized. If there are musicians and singers enough, then an orchestra and choir my be constituted. However, the organizing of these church departments should not be hastened but should be allowed to develop normally and easily as the church grows and expands.

If it is wise that there be a written standard for church membership, it is also wise that there be a constitution and by-laws adopted by the whole church membership. This will be their rule and guide in the government of their church. It will make for a clear understanding in all business matters. When there is this written rule by which the pastor, the board, and the people can conduct themselves in all matters pertaining to the business of the church, there results beautiful harmony and smooth working in the entire church program. The constitution should consist of about six articles as follows: name, purpose, membership, officers, meetings, and amendments. The by-laws should provide detailed instructions for the election of officers (these will include their qualifications), duties of officers, and conduct of meetings, further regulations concerning church membership, finances of the church, organization and operation

[ 135 ]

of its various departments, and any other matters which need to be specified. The constitution should be made difficult to be amended, while the by-laws should be subject to amendment by a two-thirds vote at any regular meeting of the congregation.

The question arises, Should there be a board of elders in the church? Deacons, we know, are Scriptural; but does not the Bible also refer to there being *elders* in the local churches? Acts 14:23 says, "And when they had ordained them elders in every church, and had prayed with fasting, they commended them to the Lord, on whom they believed." James 5:14-15 instructs that when one is sick he should call for the *elders* of the church. Paul said to Timothy, "Let the *elders* that rule well be counted of double honor, especially they who labor in the Word and doctrine." 1 Tim. 5:17. To Titus also he said (Titus 1:5), "Ordain *elders* in every city." From Miletus Paul sent to Ephesus and called the *elders* of the church. Acts 20:17. From these passages it seems that there is abundant Scriptural precedent for elders in the church. What about this?

It will also be seen by the examination of the Scriptures that an elder is a minister of the gospel. Peter declared, "The elders among you I exhort, who also am an elder . . . feed the flock of God which is among you . . . and when the Chief Shepherd shall appear, ye shall receive a crown of glory." 1 Peter 5:1-4. Without doubt Peter was a preacher

[ 136 ]

and an apostle of the highest order. He is instructing ministers to feed the flock, etc. He says he is an elder and is exhorting elders. Therefore surely an elder is a minister. When John wrote his second and third epistles he called himself an elder. 2 John 1; 3 John 1. With reference to the elders in Acts 11:30; 15:2, 4, 6, 22, 23; 16:4; 20:17, 28; 21:18, it appears clearly, and particularly from Titus 1:2, 5 and 7, that the words "elder" and "bishop" are synonymous and both refer to ordained ministers and leaders in the church. It would seem that the word "elder" refers to the man and the word "bishop" or "overseer" refers to the office which he holds. It can be taken therefore that an elder is an ordained minister.

The conclusion from the two paragraphs above, then, is this: In the early churches there was a plurality of elders. That is to say, each church had a number of ordained men who served as its pastors. The question follows, Is this then not a Scriptural precedent and pattern? Should not we also in these days have several ordained men as pastors of our churches? Before accepting this conclusion, let us be reminded of certain other things. In the days of the apostles Paul and Peter there was no New Testament as yet and thus no fixed standard of gospel truth by which all mooted questions could be settled. The church was in the process of receiving this revelation from God. In order to safeguard that truth and to save it from "private interpretation" (2 Peter 1:20), it was the plan of God that there be a group of Holy

Ghost men in each church who would compare their divine impressions and together determine the thought and mind of God concerning His truth for the church. Also in this formative period the business of being a pastor was entirely new to all concerned and there was need for the development of many such workers according to the proper standard. By their association with each other they shared the ministry of the early churches, were able to observe the practice of each other, and thus all of them learned simultaneously. This rapidly developed those leaders of the churches who doubtless later were able to assume greater responsibilities and the task of establishing new churches and creating new elders and deacons. That there was a distinction in the rank of these elders is implied in 1 Tim. 5:17, where it is stated that some labored in word and in doctrine. This would indicate a senior and a subordinate capacity. Some may have labored in the caring for the poor, and others in the music, or personal visitation and similar pastoral functions. That they were supported by the church also is indicated by 1 Tim. 5:17, 18 where Timothy was reminded that the laborer was worthy of his reward.

Today we have a complete revelation of the will of God in the canonized New Testament. Hence a release from the necessity of the plurality of elders for that purpose. Also by our practice of associate and assistant pastors in a number of our larger churches, and the varied ministry which evangelists, Bible conventions, and visiting ministers give us today, there is that diversity of ministry which the early church received by its plurality of elders. The great need for extending the gospel as rapidly as possible into all the world surely justifies us in spreading our forces as far as they will go without weakening our home churches. Likewise the development of our deacon boards to serve in something of a spiritual capacity as well as for the original purpose for which the deacons were chosen (Acts 6:1-7), strengthens the hands of the local pastor and enables one man alone to be the elder of a local church. It seems that these considerations abundantly justify and render God-approved the practice of the present-day church of having one pastor only, dispensing with a plurality of elders. Our conclusion therefore would be that, although there were many elders in the early churches, it is not God's will that there be a board of elders in our present-day churches. By no means should there be a board of senior laymen who are called elders, for this is and always has been un-Scriptural.

# CHAPTER 10

## *Church Administration*

CHURCH organization is setting up the machinery of local church government. Church administration is operating that machinery. Some claim that it is easier to set up an organization than it is to operate it. But surely the wisdom which would equip one to constitute on organization that is Scriptural ought to be sufficient to enable one to look after the administration of the organization. However, it must be admitted that the patience required for looking after the detailed functioning, repairing of broken parts, and continued using of a machine many times is lacking in the genius of a man who was able to construct it in the first place. Be these things as they may, it nevertheless is absolutely necessary that a church not only be organized well but that it be administered efficiently and faithfully.

As the organization of a church begins with its membership so the administration that matters most in church has to do with its membership. A standard of membership is erected and a definite membership is constituted. Now let the pastor see that the adopted standard of membership is adhered to and that the line of demarkation between members and non-members is kept clear and distinct. Keep your membership clean. Keep your membership list up to date. As soon as events take place which require it, remove from your rolls those who have died or moved to another city. The latter can be placed in an inactive file if there is a possibility of their absence being only temporary.

Concerning those who backslide or fall below the standard for membership, particular attention must be given them. The instructions in Matt. 18:15-17 given by our Lord should be followed. Gal. 6:1 is also a scripture to be observed. "Brethren, if a man be overtaken in a fault, ye which are spiritual, restore such an one in the spirit of meekness; considering thyself, lest thou also be tempted." It is the task of the servant of the Lord in meekness to instruct those that oppose. "In meekness instructing those that oppose themselves; if God peradventure will give them repentance to the acknowledging of the truth; and that they may recover themselves out of the snare of the devil, who are taken captive by him at his will." 2 Tim. 2:25-26. After serious, loving, prayerful, Godlike persistence in seeking to win them back, it may become necessary at last to take disciplinary measures and either suspend them from membership (2 Thess. 3:6, 14, 15) or expel them. 1 Cor. 5:2, 13. This action should not be taken singlehandedly but in consultation with one's deacon board. However, there should be no negligence and weakness in such matters, for God is a holy God and He very definitely rebuked the church at Pergamos for having among them those that held the doctrine of Balaam, and the church at Thyatira for suffering that woman Jezebel to teach. Rev. 2:14, 20. The Lord does not wink at sin in local churches. He commended the church at Ephesus that they could not bear them which were evil. Rev. 2:2.

The business management of the church should be efficient and thorough. Some pastors are like the man who builded upon the sand, with regard to the management of their church business matters. The ownership of the property in which they worship is left in jeopardy. To have the church deeded to certain individuals even as trustees and not to specify that it is to "them or their successors in office" is to run the serious risk of having these individuals die, backslide, change their doctrinal views, or move so far away that they cannot be conveniently contacted. This renders the task of securing their signatures extremely difficult in the case of the sale or the mortgaging of the building. Nobody should ever be made a trustee for life, and the deed should indicate that such and such men are trustees only as long as they hold that office according to the constitution and by-laws of the church. This enables the church to keep its trustee board up to date and give them instructions as to its desires. The name of the church as it appears in the deed should likewise be identical in every detail with the incorporated name of the church or its official name as indicated in the constitution. This will save confusion and avoid the shadow on the title which a neglect of this measure will constitute.

Deeds should be registered and properly recorded at the court house. In so doing, if there should be an accidental loss of the original deed, a certified copy could be secured. It is the part of wisdom to keep all important documents (deeds, insurance papers, and the like) in a fireproof vault or in a safe deposit box at the bank. By no means let them be kept somewhere in a desk or in the hands of some official who might feel his importance in having the deeds and possibly refuse to relinquish them when requested to do so, or when there is some question about his continuance in office. The secretary is the official custodian of the deeds of the church and all similar documents. The pastor should have access to them at all times.

The question arises concerning the need and use of trustees in connection with church property. Property cannot be owned by a group of people, unless incorporated, until trustees have been appointed. With a corporation, its board of directors are considered its trustees. If the church is not entitled to be set in order in a Scriptural sense, not having men eligible for election as deacons, it will be necessary to constitute a trustee board in order to purchase and own property. The pastor of the church, one business man from the worshipers there, and a district officer (either presbyter or superintendent) could be constituted as trustees. Or a group of three laymen could be chosen from the brethren of the prospective church. A constitution and by-laws should be drafted at the very same time (whether or not the church is set in order), in order that there may be rules governing the tenure of office of these trustees, their duties, powers, etc. If there is a church membership, and elections are held annually, and there is as yet no deacon board, it is suggested that one trustee be elected for three years, one for two years and another for one year, their successors being elected for three-year terms. Trustees, of course, serve as representatives of the congregation only in the matter of the ownership of the property. It is they who will sign if a mortgage is given or if the property is sold. *They do not have spiritual functions and powers as church officers.* As soon as a Scripturally qualified deacon board can be constituted, whose duties will include material as well as spiritual things, it is evident that there is no longer need of a separate trustee board. The deacons can serve as trustees. A multiplying of church boards is confusing and it is unwise to have more machinery than is necessary.

The matter of church finances is naturally an important one. The apostle Paul was careful, when he took the contribution of the Gentile churches to the poor saints at Jerusalem, that no blame should be attached to him nor suspicion aroused by his handling of this fund. 2 Cor. 8:20, 21. He has instructed us, too, to provide things honest in the sight of all men. Rom. 12:17. If all things are naked and open unto the eyes of Him with whom we have to do (Heb. 4:13), then it seems consistent that we should have all our business matters open and aboveboard. Church finances are the church's business and, as a matter of fact, the church's own doings. It is not only that each man is entitled to know what he himself (through his agents) is doing, but good business principles require it. A treasurer elected by the church should receive all offerings, make careful record of every receipt, and then bank the money every week. As offerings are taken morning and evening or at any service, a count of the money should be made by more than one person, and the amount turned over to the treasurer with a written notation as to how much it is. The treasurer's bookkeeping should be accurate and according to approved methods. A multi-column cash book is convenient for smaller churches in which a number of accounts can be kept simultaneously. If an individual record of the offering of every giver is required (presupposing the use of the envelope system), then it would be wise to open a regular ledger with an account for each giver. The one thing needful is to keep a careful set of books that can be audited or certified by an auditor. Such an auditing once a year, by the way, is an excellent thing. It calls in impartial, disinterested, professional men who will make a fair investigation of financial matters and give certification that all is correct and above reproach. The church owes it to itself and to its treasurer to secure this certification once a year.

Concerning the pastor's salary, there is much that could and should be said. First, as to the manner in which he is paid, the method that is used will naturally vary depending on the size of the church. In the home mission work which is not set in order or where there are no officers or even church membership, there would be no objection to the pastor's receiving directly and personally all the offerings. From this he must pay all expenses and trust the Lord for what he will need in addition. However, as the church assumes definite form and membership, and particularly if it is set in order with a deacon board, the time has arrived for an accounting to be made of the monies which are given. This will instill within the hearts of the people a sense of responsibility for the pastor's support. The amount will doubtless still be quite small and its being reported will stimulate further giving on the part of the people. It is therefore recommended that a treasurer be elected who should handle the monies, possibly giving the entire amount to the pastor for his support. When other church obligations are assumed and expenses incurred, either a certain offering could be designated for that purpose (a Sunday night or a week-night offering), or else the needed amount be raised by private subscription.

The time will come in the growth of the church when a more definite arrangement should be made concerning the support of the pastor. It is the practice in some sections for the board to arrange with the pastor that he should receive a certain percentage of the total offerings taken in. This could be 90%, 75%, 66%, or 50%, dependent upon the volume of offerings received. Another plan is for the pastor to receive a certain basic salary each Sunday (say $35), and at the end of the month for him to receive a stated share of all the income in excess of his salary. These plans enable the pastor's salary to rise and fall along with the income of the church. They recognize that he is responsible for its income and let him suffer or profit by his failure or success. Another plan is for the pastor to be given a definite salary from week to week.

If possible, it is well that the church should provide a parsonage for their pastor. They could also pay utility bills and the expense of operating his car. This relieves him from anxiety about his income and enables him to devote all his thought and attention to the spiritual problems which lie so heavily upon him. His salary should be determined by the extent of the responsibilities which rest upon him, and also by comparison with the salaries of men who occupy similar positions in the secular world, some thought being given as to how it compares with the salaries of those to whom he ministers. His people remember that the general tone and self-respect of the whole church is gauged by their pastor's standing and by the material provision which is made for him by them. Let the deacons and the people be glad to provide for their pastor that which will give him the standing which he and his church deserve in the community.

On the other hand, it is reprehensible and dangerous spiritually for the pastor to be avaricious. It is specifically stated in his qualifications that he must not be greedy of filthy lucre. 1 Tim. 3:3; 1 Peter 5:12. The warning concerning the love of money (in 1 Tim. 6:9, 10) is applicable to ministers as well as to laymen. A pastor must keep unwaveringly before him the gilt-edged promise of His master that if he seeks first the kingdom of God and His righteousness all these (material) things shall be added unto him. Matt. 6:33. He must learn and hold steadfastly to the lesson which Paul records in Phil. 4:10-19; namely, to be content in whatsoever state one is, whether it is to be abased or to abound, to be full or to be hungry. If the servant of the Lord cannot trust his Master to look after his material needs, then he does not have sufficient faith in the cause in which he is engaged to justify his continuing therein. If his eyes are upon money he might properly be called an hireling rather than a shepherd.

But whatever the pastor's salary, and in whatever way he receives it, let there always be a full report to his congregation concerning it. As a matter of fact, not only should all church finances be handled in a business-like fashion, but careful reporting of them should be made to the church periodically. A few think it wise to make a weekly report from the pulpit, or on a bulletin board prominently displayed. Others prefer to make a monthly report. A quarterly report is a method followed in some churches. Once a year, at the very least, there should be a full and complete reporting of all monies received and paid out.

The place of the official board in the administration of the church is a very prominent one. In another chapter we will present in detail the qualifications and duties of the deacons. Here we will comment upon the installation of the deacons and the conduct of their meetings. After the election of the deacons each year it is wise as well as Scriptural that there be a public consecration or dedication service. When the first deacons were chosen they were set before the apostles, who prayed and laid their hands upon them. Acts 6:6. It may not be necessary or wise for the pastor to lay hands upon the deacons that are chosen to work with him, but he should formally accept them from the congregation as their gift to him, and should lead them in a prayer of consecration for their task. This gives them full standing and recognition by the congregation, and also shows that the pastor definitely accepts them as his official board and welcomes them into this close relationship to himself.

Following this public service, at a convenient time, the first meeting can be held with this board. If the congregation has not specified which of the board is to serve as secretary, and which as treasurer (according to its constitution and bylaws), then the first meeting of the board should take care of the choice of these officers. If the constitution so allows, the board may choose some who have not been elected as deacons, if advisable. The secretary of the church, if elected by the church, is not necessarily the secretary of the official board. The church secretary, if elected by the church, will be the custodian of all documents of importance, etc., whereas the secretary of the official board will take the minutes of the meetings of that board. It is more convenient, of course, to have one person serve in both capacities. It is not advisable to have a chairman of the board other than the pastor, nor even an assistant chairman. There will be no need for such as long as there is a pastor in the church; and in the interim between pastors they can appoint a chairman pro tem or the secretary could serve in that capacity.

There should be regular meetings of the official board. It is a mockery to elect a man to a position and not give him an opportunity to serve in that position. It is suggested that there be a meeting of the official board at least once each month unless some unusual situation prevents. This should be held whether or not there is specific business to come before them. There is always need for fellowship and counsel together and a time of earnest prayer for the welfare of the church. Minutes should be kept of all notions passed at each meeting and it would be well for the secretary to record a brief statement concerning various discussions engaged in whether or not they climax in a properly passed resolution.

In addition to the meetings of the official board, it will be necessary for the pastor to meet with other committees of his congregation. There are the officers of the Sunday School with whom he must confer, and he must be present at the weekly or monthly meeting of the Sunday School teachers and workers. If there is a young people's group, he is automatically a member of their executive committee. He must remember that "ex officio" does not mean "honorary" but "by virtue of his office." That is to say, he should not consider it merely his privilege to attend such meetings, but his duty as well. He is the head of every department of his church, as well as of the church as a whole. His purpose in attending these meetings is to contribute his counsel and exert his influence for spiritual wisdom and aggressiveness. His presence should not overshadow or in any wise intimidate others, and he should not take from them the responsibility of work which is rightly theirs. He should value their wisdom and counsel and encourage initiative on their part. He should never go over the head of his subordinates in making arrangements concerning details that are rightfully under the care of these subordinates. If he has any suggestions to make, let him do it to the officer in charge, and have that officer contact the member involved.

[ 151 ]

Before we consider the matter of the annual business meeting, let us take up the question of the election of the pastor. There are a number of methods which may be followed. Let us notice first that very rare situation in which the pastor has it decreed in the constitution and by-laws that he should remain the pastor for life. The only situation that could be more unwise, in this connection, is the arrangement (which very seldom occurs) in which the pastor is allowed also to name his successor. This is commonly considered the limit of self-preservation and self-seeking, and is a rather practical demonstration of "lording it over God's heritage." Can this be reconciled with the spirit of the Master who laid down His life for the sheep; or with the scripture, "He that loveth his life shall lose it"? John 12:25.

The matter is now resolved to one of two methods: to be elected for an indefinite period, or to be voted on year after year. Which of these methods is correct or better? To be elected indefinitely has its advantages. It gives the pastor a settled feeling, and also gives him time in which to work out a long-range program. It is true that a pastor cannot really get started in an effective program in less than two or three years' time. He will need at least one year in which to get acquainted with his own members, if his assembly is large, especially to learn of their abilities as workers or prospective workers. Another year or two will be needed to get acquainted with the people of the town or city. He can then begin working to a definite plan, using the material that he has on hand. We do not imply by this that he should not attempt anything constructive until after a few years, but rather that he is not thoroughly conversant with the local staff or situation until he has had time to get fully acquainted with them. If he has been called for an indefinite time it will enable him to get this information and adjustment which he needs and then really build for God. Also an indefinite call to a pastor eliminates the yearly election at which there sometimes are agitators who take advantage of the fact to stir dissatisfaction in the church. Likewise intelligent planning requires that arrangements be made at least a year ahead if one is to secure capable evangelists, be ready for next summer's Vacation Bible School, etc. It is either presumption on the part of the pastor to plan beyond the time of his election, or neglect on his part if he does not plan far enough ahead. These are the reasons why a pastor should be called indefinitely.

On the other hand, there are disadvantages to being called indefinitely. A pastor might assume that he is called for life. He succumbs to the indolence within his nature, rests on his oars, and coasts along without earnestly applying himself toward pastoral success. This is grievous and hurtful. A pastor thus called might feel that he was entrenched so safely that none would be able to oust him, and he therefore could be less careful than he otherwise would be about maintaining friends and goodwill. This would be a regrettable result of one's election for an indefinite time. Also there are many pastors who prefer to have an annual showdown or revelation as to how they actually stand with their people. They say they would not want to continue as pastor if they were unwanted by their people. The only way to know absolutely how one stands is by a secret ballot test.

There are modifications also of these two systems, providing for a two-year term of office, or for re-election after the first and second years and then an indefinite tenure following that.

It will be necessary for each pastor and board to choose that plan which fits their local situation and the nature and desire of the pastor himself. God will give wisdom and indicate the plan which will be right for the occasion.

While considering the term of office of the pastor, let us also look at the question of how long deacons should serve. Confusion may have come into the minds of some by the comparison of deacons with trustees. It is the customary legal procedure that a board of trustees should serve for staggered terms, one or two going out of office each year and their successors being elected for three-year terms. This is to avoid too rapid a turnover in the signatures of those who are legal representatives of the church in the owning of their property. A different situation prevails in connection with deacons. These are men who, in addition to their material responsibility, must have exemplary characters and measure up to a high standard of spiritual excellence as set forth in the Word of God. 1 Tim. 3:8-13. It is possible that a deacon should fall below the standard within one year's time. To retain him in office for another two years would be a blemish and handicap for the church. To have some arrangement whereby he could be removed from office would also create a certain amount of unpleasantness. Likewise there is the possibility that some other man will qualify as a deacon in the meantime and become more desirable than one now occupying the position. To deny the church the opportunity of the election of this man (or more than one such person) until a long term of office for the incumbent deacons has expired would be manifestly a handicap. In many churches the pastor himself is subject to re-election every year. Why should his subordinate officers be elected for a longer term than he? For these reasons it is recommended that deacons be elected for a term of one year, subject to re-election. Some think it wise to insert a provision here that, after say three successive years of service, a deacon is not eligible for re-election until one year has gone by. The motive here is to make necessary the election of new material by way of at least a tryout of such material. This advantage may be outweighed by the loss of the services of a faithful and efficient servant of the church.

Now for our consideration of the annual business meeting. This is a matter of great importance. There is a certain custom which is productive of evil rather than of good. That custom is to allow the members of the church to discuss and decide details of business which properly belong to the official board. The services of the janitor and his salary, for instance, or details concerning what should be provided for the pastor. Even the question of the pastor's salary itself is a matter which could easily and properly be taken care of by the official board and the pastor. To do otherwise encourages personal comments which inevitably produce feelings and counter-remarks and the net result is damage and ill will. Let the annual business meeting be a time for the election of church officers, the presentation of reports of the church accomplishments of the year, and the discharge of any business which legally requires the action of the entire church.

There will be, first of all, the election of the pastor if that is provided for in the bylaws or according to arrangements made with him. His election, and the election of all officers for that matter, should be by secret ballot. Certainly there should be no ratification by a show of hands or standing to one's feet. How extremely difficult it would be to get a negative vote under such an arrangement! How unfair to the people to be required, bluntly and rudely, almost personally, to affront an individual in order to express a vote against him! A secret ballot preserves absolute freedom of will and secures as accurate an expression of the will of the people as is possible

The practice of using a nominating committee has its advantages and disadvantages. If a nominating committee is appointed by the pastor, then there is the temptation to control them and influence their report. If they are elected by the people this would involve an interval of time between their election and their report for they must have time to meet and prepare their report. The nominating committee should not be given the power to bring in a slate of officers naming only one candidate for each office. Furthermore, if they bring in two or more candidates for each office, the presiding officer should make it clear that nominations from the floor also are always in order. Accepted parliamentary practice provides for this and it is a constitutional American right. The advantage in having a nominating committee is that a small group can frankly talk over qualifications for office in a way that would be disquieting and personal if it were done in open session. If a nominating committee would be impartial and uninfluenced by personal considerations of any kind, then it would be more effective to have such a committee. It is going to have to be decided by each church whether or not it is wise to have a nominating committee.

The alternative procedure to having a nominating committee is that the first ballot should be considered a nominating ballot. The tellers should bring back to the floor the names of the candidates placing them on a blackboard. If the voters so agree, only the names of those having the greatest number of votes may be placed on the board. From these names therefore let the people vote again until a sufficient number have received a majority vote of all votes cast. To elect by a plurality vote (the high candidate) is quite faulty since it is by no means certain that he is the real desire of the people or would receive a majority vote if he were placed in opposition to one other candidate.

Tellers may be appointed by the chairman but their appointment should be ratified by a vote of the people. The laws of some states require this and it would be good if all business meetings were conducted thus. The report of the teller committee is accepted as prima facie evidence that votes were cast as reported.

Another item of business at the annual business meeting is the reports made by the pastor, secretary, treasurer, and other department heads. It would be helpful if these reports could be written out and mimeographed in advance and a copy presented to each member present. They could then be read aloud by the pastor, or someone appointed by him, and carefully noted and observed by all present. Here is the occasion for the thorough setting forth of the financial status of the church. Receipts and offerings in some detail should be reported. A balance sheet of assets and liabilities is also of interest and value. There should be reported more particularly the spiritual progress and development of the church. Give the number of active members and inactive ones, those received during the past year, etc. Tell how many have been saved, filled with the Spirit, baptized in water, etc. in the past year. State how many pastoral calls the pastor and his assistants have made. Report the revivals, special services, radio, and institutional work which have been conducted during the past year. There should be a report of the Sunday School, too. Compare this with the report of a year ago. Comparative charts and tables are likewise helpful. A statement could also be made at the annual business meeting concerning any plans for the future that may have matured at that time. This can be a time of general inventory and stock-taking, lifting up one's Ebenezer and citing one's goal for the new year. All of these things are most wholesome, inspiring to the church, and glorifying to God.

# CHAPTER II

## Departments and Agencies

AS a church grows and develops, the pastor will be faced with the responsibility of administering its various departments and agencies. Foremost among these is his *Sunday School*. This is distinctively the teaching department of the church, as well as that function that cares particularly for the young of the flock. These are two solemn charges which the Lord has given his pastors and they must be devoutly obeyed. Every member of the church should come to Sunday School if physically able. The Sunday School enrollment should exceed the church enrollment; for it has the church membership as a base, to which may be added many who are not even saved, as well as children who are too young for church membership. The Sunday School should be carefully organized. Its teachers should be trained and efficient. It should have its own working plans for visiting its absentees and enlarging its membership. A Home Department and a Cradle Roll Department are extension phases of the Sunday School which are important and valuable. Let the pastor study thoroughly the whole art and science of successful Sunday School work. Let him pray hard and work hard for the constant improvement and growth of his Sunday School. Let him not consider that this is a mere auxiliary of his church work, or an appendage tacked on for tradition's sake. His is the ultimate responsibility for the success or failure of his school. He must not fail.

A *Vacation Bible School* is the conducting of daily school sessions in the church during vacation time, continuing from Monday through Friday, for three hours each morning. Schools are usually conducted either for two or three weeks, the latter being preferable. Every available member of your church can find a ministry in the Vacation Bible School. Skill and experience are not necessarily needed in order to be a worker here. There is room for Bible teachers, an art teacher, a music teacher, a recreation director, as well as secretaries, treasurers, storytellers, memory-work teachers, pianists, and helpers who have only to sit with the children. Drivers of cars and busses likewise are needed. There is a job for everyone. Here is an excellent place not only to have two or three weeks of intensive Bible indoctrination of our children and to witness a wonderful revival among them, but also to give everyone who will accept it a place of ministry for the Lord, and to discover many hidden talents in the church membership. Here also is an opportunity for the exercise and development of real executive ability in the leaders of this school.

It is really not a newfangled idea to conduct *Children's Churches* once a week. This is a distinct carrying out of Christ's commands, "Feed My lambs," and "Suffer the little children to come unto Me." These are church sessions held just for the little folk themselves, under intermediate age. Primary and Junior children are so different from adults in their expressions and sphere of life that they need to have church worship adjusted to their level. A service conducted for them should be somewhat on the pattern of a regular service but should be about things with which the children are familiar. It should be in their language and concerning their problems. Stories, motion songs, and exercises are more acceptable and profitable to them than the long sermon for adults ever could be. Let there be plenty of action, blackboard drawing, object lessons, and flannelgraph work—not just for amusement, but as a means of spiritual education of the children. Let them learn through eye-gate as well as ear-gate and this will not be tedious or tiresome. How richly fruitful are these sessions with the little ones, inculcating into their deepest nature and life love for God, faith in the Lord Jesus, and obedience to His commands. Little missionaries can be molded so easily at this early age. Tithe paying can be introduced and become a firm habit. The evils of the classroom and public school association can likewise be counteracted by this wholesome church worship period in the house of God.

In addition to these departments for children there are also two other agencies which can be used to the same laudable end. We refer to *Weekday Religious Instruction* and what is known as *Bible Clubs,* or Bible study hours. In practically all large cities school authorities are willing to release the children for one period in the week to attend a class conducted in a neighborhood church. Here the basic facts of religion are taught. This is also called Released Time or Week-day Christian Education. It is the usual policy for the various churches of the city to co-operate in such a program. Children whose parents request it, are released to attend the church of their own preference. As the children are transferred to the church building (it is the obligation of the church to provide conveyance, if such is needed), the pastor and his workers can follow any curriculum which they think wise. This is a priceless opportunity for the pastor and his workers to instil into the hearts of these little children the wonderful truths of God's Word. It is by all means desirable that pastors should take advantage of their opportunities in this matter and press their petition that the schools of their city shall release the children for this Weekday Religious Instruction.

The story hours or Bible clubs have developed out of the practice of some enterprising and evangelistic-hearted pastors who held weekly meetings for children in the city parks or other available outdoor places. These were conducted in Children's Church fashion with object lessons, short stories, etc. When cold weather came and the children had to go back to public school, those delightful sessions, rather than being discontinued, were transferred to some indoor home parlors that were friendly to them. In the various parts of the city these story-hour sessions are held all through the winter, preferably on Friday afternoons. Where a large enough staff is available, a number of these children's services are conducted simultaneously. They are means of Bible indoctrination and real evangelism, and are feeders for the church and Sunday School. Let us use every means available—"if by any means we might save some."

Returning now to the more commonly known and better established departments of a church, let us consider the organization of the *Young People*. The purpose of the young people's association is to provide fellowship for those of the same age, compatibility in worship, and opportunity for training and Christian service. Young people should elect their own officers and conduct their own meetings. To have a sponsor from among the mature and most spiritual workers of the church is proper and acceptable but in any event the responsibility for conducting their own services and all their outside activities should rest wholly upon the young people. Their first objective should be to contribute to the success of the activities of the church of which they are members. They should sing in its choir, play in its orchestra, teach in its Sunday School, and attend its services as regularly as any adult member. With the pastor of the church as a father and elder brother among them, they should find spiritual exercise and growth in their young people's association.

There may also be a number of children in a church who are too young for the Young People's Society and too old for the Children's Church. These should be encouraged and assisted in constituting a little class or association of their own, called by some convenient title. They will need definite adult sponsorship and leadership more than the young people, but their talents and abilities should be developed. They should be encouraged to give sermonettes, conduct the song service, testify for the Lord, play special musical numbers, serve as promotion secretaries to increase the membership of their group and do aggressive evangelistic work among schoolmates and other children of their own age. We must do all we can to hold and train children of every age.

A large part of the worship of the congregation is occupied with *music* of various kinds. Congregational singing, choir work, special vocal numbers, full orchestra and band, ensembles, and individual instrumental numbers—all of these under the leadership of the choir leader and band director or a minister of music—are a great and important phase of church activity. If the church is large enough there will be occasion for the organization of these musical departments. There can, of course, be overlapping here with the other groups who serve as departments of the church. The pastor is fortunate who has, either in his congregation or available, an individual who is qualified to serve as a trainer and leader of musicians. An assistant pastor who may be qualified in this regard is of real assistance to the pastor in this ministry. This position requires not only musical training and ability but also a standard of holiness at least equal to that of other members of the church. It needs a pleasing personality and ability to lead and inspire others. The pastor would do well to give much prayer and attention to securing the leadership which is needed here. There will naturally come the temptation to secure the services of one outside of the church membership who would have the necessary musical qualifications but who might fall short of the spiritual requisite. Let the pastor beware of this pitfall. Far better to secure one with less musical ability but who can serve as a real example in a spiritual way to those whom he leads in singing or playing instruments.

Turning now from a study of church departments, let us consider some of the means for gospel propagation which are available to the present-day pastor. Foremost among these is the time-honored revival meeting. From the "protracted meeting" of a previous generation to the evangelistic campaign of today, the church has continually used the policy of a night-after-night series of evangelistic services in its effort to revive the church and to save the lost. Two or three of these special efforts each year would seem to provide a more balanced program of church activity than a year-long succession of revivals without time for the Bible-teaching ministry of the pastor or a training class for his Sunday School workers. The pastor should make careful preparation for each revival both by extensive advertising and much prayer. Neighborhood prayer meetings and special prayer services in the church are productive of faith, interest, and answer to prayer in the success of the revival campaign. The training of personal workers and their activity during the revival contribute to its success. The name and address of each convert should be secured and a careful follow-up system faithfully pursued in order to conserve the results.

For year-round gospel propagation, there is available to most pastors the radio, the modern miracle of communication. Jesus said, "What I tell you in darkness that speak ye in light, and what you hear in the ear preach ye upon the housetops." Matt. 10:27. This may not have reference to the radio, but it does justify us in proclaiming from the housetops (or radio broadcasting towers) that which He has whispered into our hearts concerning His life and power. If the Lord has told us to go tell—and He has—and if radio is an efficient means of telling— and it is—then how can we escape the conclusion that it is the will of God for us to use the radio as much as we can for the proclamation of the glad tidings of the gospel? Radio preaching and gospel broadcasting are a distinct ministry within themselves. The employment of the best possible technique and conformity to the ethics of the broadcasting field are highly advisable as one engages in this type of ministry. Give to the world your very best when you get on the air. Better not broadcast at all than send forth that which will reflect poorly on you, your church, and your message.

*House-to-house visitation*, neighborhood or city-wide canvasses, and thorough distribution of full gospel literature cannot be less than the will of God for the pastor. The Sanhedrin accused the disciples of "filling Jerusalem with their doctrine." Acts 5:28. Can we be similarly accused? Would to God that we were so full of the Holy Ghost, so impelled to tell the message everywhere, so zealous for the conversion of souls and imparting this divine, blessed, old-time gospel everywhere that we would not cease until we filled our parishes with our message. Luke 8:1 tells us that Jesus "went throughout every city and village preaching and showing the glad tidings of the kingdom of God." Concerning the apostles also it is recorded in Acts 5:42, "And daily in the temple, and *in every house*, they ceased not to teach and preach Jesus Christ." Paul the apostle was neither too important nor too busy to do house-to-house canvassing, as is plainly recorded in Acts 20:20.

*Tract and gospel-paper* distribution by the members of your church, through boxes in bus stations and railroad depots, at street meetings, church services, etc., is another effective means of gospel propagation. He has told us, "In the morning sow thy seed, and in the evening withhold not thine hand: for thou knowest not whether shall prosper, either this or that, or whether they shall be alike good." Eccl. 11:6.

Another means which is available to us in these days for the preaching of the unsearchable riches of Christ is *newspaper advertising*. Newspapers go into practically every home in our cities every day. We can have one hundred times as great an audience in this way as we ever can have in our churches. Needless to say, there are art and ethics in newspaper advertising as well as in radio broadcasting. A little common sense and willingness to conform to the desires of newspaper editors will give us an entree to them, win their friendship, and open wide this door of effectual gospel ministry. Who says we should not do this? Our Master said, "Preach the gospel to every creature." The apostle Paul had as his objective "to make all men see what is the fellowship of the mystery, which from the beginning of the world hath been hid in God, who created all things by Jesus Christ." If we obey Christ's command with Paul's fervent spirit we will utilize every possible means for the spreading of the gospel story.

We cannot omit reference to *outdoor and institutional work* which every aggressive pastor has upon his schedule. In most municipalities, permission can be secured for conducting street services. During the summer months this is the ideal outlet of ministry, not only for your Spirit-filled men and women but for your young people's society as well. The pastor himself should blaze the trail here, make all arrangements, and set the pattern for carrying on these meetings. Leadership can be transferred to some other church worker if the pastor himself must be released for other ministry that would conflict. Once a week or once a month a squad could visit the city or county jail and county home or boys' reformatory and whatever hospitals were accessible. The Lord's love knows no bounds and it reaches behind prison bars and into the sickbeds and rooms of all kinds of institutions.

A thoughtful, efficient administration of church affairs will require the pastor to plan far in advance the schedule which he is to follow throughout the year. Definite sessions should be reserved for revival services. If one is to secure evangelists that have been successful on the field, then it is necessary to invite them many months ahead of time. There is also the planning for the Vacation Bible School each summer. It is poor business to await the late spring to make preparations for this big event. It is far better to have the executive officers of this school assigned their tasks at least six months ahead of the time when school is to be held. Much preliminary planning and many business meetings must be held in preparation for a successful Vacation Bible School. The Sunday School likewise has its yearly schedule of elections, promotions, adjustments of staff personnel, Christmas program, Easter climax, etc. All of these need intelligent planning far in advance. The summer season for street work, any desired opening of branch schools, and meetings held in nearby towns should be thought out carefully well ahead of time. Thus it can be seen that at least one year's work must be in the mind and heart of the capable pastor.

# CHAPTER 12

## Buildings and Equipment

CONCERNING church buildings and equipment something needs to be said. The prophet Haggai gave instructions to the people of God to "go up to the mountain, and bring wood, and build the house." Hag. 1:8. He said that God's curse was upon the yield of their harvest "because of Mine house that is waste, and ye run every man unto his own house." Hag. 1:9. As the house of God was completed, the blessing of the Lord was pronounced upon it—"The glory of this latter house shall be greater than of the former, saith the Lord of hosts, and in this place will I give peace." Hag. 2:9. There came a time when the sons of the prophet said unto Elisha, "Behold, now, the place where we dwell with thee is too strait for us." 2 Kings 6:1. They asked that they might go and build a larger place, and Elisha consented and went with them to their task. Solomon built a house that was very great—"For great is our God and above all gods." 2 Chron. 2:5. "And it came to pass, when the priests were come out of the holy place, that the cloud filled the house of the Lord, so that the priests could not stand to minister because of the cloud: for the glory of the Lord had filled the house of the Lord." 1 Kings 8:10, 11.

It is true that, when Jacob awakened after his dream of the ladder into heaven, he declared, "Surely the Lord is in this place, and I knew it not. And he was afraid and said, How dreadful is this place! This is none other but the house of God." Gen. 28:16, 17. There was nothing here but the stone that he had used for his pillow which he set up as a pillar and poured oil upon. It is the presence of God that makes a house of God. On the other hand, it is of divine record that God's children built Him tabernacles and temples in which He was pleased to dwell.

It is a matter of common sense to know that our bodies require accommodation and comfort if we are to sit at ease and give attention to matters of the soul and spirit. As our bodies themselves are vehicles in which our spiritual natures are contained, so the church buildings in which we worship are a necessary means to a spiritual end. It is not advised that large fortunes be invested in an attempt to imitate Solomon's temple when there is a dire need for consecrated funds with which to finance the carrying of the gospel to the ends of the earth. On the other hand, we ought to seek refined simplicity and beauty in the houses of worship which we erect.

[ 173 ]

The one-room church building in nearly every case is the first step toward the creating of an assembly. As the assembly increases in numbers and financial strength, it is logical and proper that better accommodations be prepared for its use. A pastor's study, prayer room, facilities for a graded Sunday School, young people's chapel, and nursery as well as a library, would be in order in the construction of a new building. Arrangements could be made for the expansion of the seating capacity of the main auditorium in case of an overflow crowd, by the inclusion of other rooms and recesses. Provision likewise should be made for the Bible class and prayer meetings which are continual functions of an operating church. Architectural plans vary according to climate, nature and contour of the ground on which the church stands, desires of the pastor and people, and their financial ability and faith. But the time has yet to be when an earnest, conscientious congregation has launched out in faith to construct a building purely for the glory of the Lord (for their convenience in doing business for God, and not merely for their own pride) and God has let them fail in the completion of their project. The Lord meets us in our active faith as we step out and attempt the necessary enlargement for the growth of His work.

It is to the glory of the Lord that our churches be equipped in that way which will contribute to the comfort and self-respect of worshipers and workers in the house of God. No family of God should be satisfied to worship in a building that is of less worth and beauty than the residences in which they live. The furniture of the house of God should compare favorably with that which is the custom of its worshipers to have in their own homes. Comfortable seats and pews, pulpit and altar furniture, chairs blackboards, maps, and all the other equipment which is necessary for efficient work, should be provided.

The outside of the building, the lawn, and general premises should be kept tidy and clean. "Man looketh on the outward appearance." God does look on the heart, but it is the natural man and men of the city whom we are seeking to win for God. They will look on the outward appearance of our church and judge us accordingly. Let us therefore be sure that there will be nothing but approval on their part for the neat and clean way in which we maintain our church premises.

An artistic and attractive church sign should be displayed on our church property. If we fail to do this it appears to be an attempt to remain anonymous, or else it is pure neglect of extending a welcome to the passer-by. A little beside the point, but related to this, is the exhortation to see that one's church is listed in the telephone directory and in the hotel lobbies of the city. It should always be an easy matter for strangers to locate our church and for everyone in the city to know where we are doing business for God.

# CHAPTER 13

## *Deacons*

T HE office of a deacon is not man's invention. The Holy Spirit Himself has decreed that there be such to serve in the Church. Acts 6:1-6 is commonly considered to be the record of the inauguration of this institution. When the early church elected a group of men to look after "the daily ministration," they elected a board which is considered to be the first deacon board ever chosen. The record of this election, the qualifications given, and the whole procedure serve as an excellent precedent for all churches to follow. Later in the growth and establishment of the early church the election of deacons became such a regular procedure that it was necessary for the Holy Spirit to provide a code or standard by which such were to be chosen. 1 Tim. 3:8-13 is such a standard and table of qualifications. It is God's own Word and final decree in this matter and must be followed implicity. In writing to the Philippians, Paul recognized that this church had both elders and deacons. Phil. 1:1. It was doubtless the practice in all of the early apostolic churches. It has been a practice down through the years and prevails among us at the present time. It is sound and Scriptural, and surely the will of God.

Before considering the qualifications and disqualifications for this office as given in the Bible let us comment upon certain factors which we may call non-qualifications. Among these are money, education, and political influence. These things should not influence pro or con in the choice of deacons. The world is influenced by these considerations because the natural, human, earthly standard is then followed. The Christian and the church must be oblivious to these considerations in making choice of a deacon. It is neither to a man's credit or to his discredit in this consideration that he is a man of money, education, or political influence. He should not be chosen on account of these things; neither should he be rejected because of them.

An examination of the Biblical standard (1 Tim. 3:8-13) reveals the following disqualifications for election as a deacon: drinking; loving money; being double tongued; having more than one wife; having a wife that is a slanderer, or not faithful in all things, or not serious. Inasmuch as the Holy Spirit has decreed that it is not good to eat flesh nor to drink wine nor anything whereby a brother stumbles or is offended or is made weak (Rom. 14:21), it is unthinkable that a man who uses intoxicating drinks in any wise should be eligible as a deacon. Being greedy of filthy lucre is considered by some as shown by the non-payment of tithes. Closely akin to this (or synonymous with it) is covetousness, which is idolatry, a sin which excludes a man even from any inheritance in the kingdom of Christ and of God. Eph. 5:5. A deacon should set a wholesome, Scriptural example in paying tithes and being generous with the money that the Lord has given him.

Being double-tongued could refer not only to downright duplicity but also to the weakness that "runs with the hares and hunts with the hounds." If a man does not have the courage of his convictions, and cannot speak out in opposition to those with whom he finds himself, and cannot be true to the pastor in the latter's absence and among those who oppose him, then he is not able to serve effectually as a deacon.

It will be of particular interest to note that wives of deacons have distinct Scriptural qualifications. They must be "grave, not slanderers, sober, faithful in all things." Slandering is speaking evil things of other people. To be grave and sober refers to their maturity and spiritual seriousness. Their faithfulness refers to their duty to their children and their husbands and in the position of a deacon's wife.

The qualifications of a deacon are found both in Acts 6 and in 1 Tim. 3. Briefly they are these: To understand the doctrines of the faith; to be full of the Holy Ghost; full of wisdom; proved over a period of time; found blameless; with a pure conscience; of good report; serious; the husband of one wife; and to rule their own houses well. The requirement that they understand the doctrines of the faith (1 Tim. 3:9) involves some maturity as a Christian, and also diligent application to the study of the Word of God. To be full of the Holy Ghost (Acts 6:3) means to have received the Baptism in the Holy Spirit. In addition to this, it means to live a Spirit-filled life according to Eph. 5:18-21. That they be full of wisdom (Acts 6:3) could refer both to business sagacity and the wisdom which comes from above. Good judgment in business matters will be required of them, so choice should be made of those who are capable along this line. The period of time which should elapse between one's conversion and eligibility for election as a deacon is needed not only to give him opportunity to study the doctrines of the faith but also to demonstrate his ability in God to live a clean, consistent, Christian life. Young converts therefore should never be elected to the office of a deacon. They should have lived a Christian life long enough to have established a good reputation and to be found blameless. Men with a pure conscience within and a clean record without can be considered good material from which deacons can be elected. The term "grave" means serious and sober-minded. This implies a sense of the importance of the issues of eternal life to which they are devoting themselves.

The requirement that a deacon should be the husband of one wife had reference to the polygamy of those days. It was the intent of the Christian church to overthrow that evil institution. It was thus demanded of ministers and deacons also that they have only one wife. It is a tragedy of civilization that the history of affairs in civilized nations must again record at this end of the age that there is a looseness along the line of matrimony. Although the possession of more than one wife at one time is not permitted legally, yet it has come to be quite popular to have a plurality of wives in another sense; that is, one at a time. In the sight of God, this is polygamy as much as the possession of many wives simultaneously. The provision that a deacon should be the husband of one wife is a statement that he should not be living with a woman if a previous wife of his is still living. The divorce evil today is as insidious as polygamy was then, and must be opposed as strongly. No man who has two living companions, or who is married to a woman in that situation, is eligible as a deacon. Furthermore the Bible declares that they must rule their children and their own houses well. This means that there must be Christian law and discipline prevailing in their homes. The deacon as a father must be the head of his household and command his children after him to obey the Lord.

We now come to the question as to how deacons should be chosen. Occasionally a pastor takes the liberty of appointing the deacons of his church. He can do this legally only if the constitution and by-laws of his church so allows. Some pastors might state publicly or privately their preference in the matter and thus strongly influence the election. It seems that such tactics are both un-Scriptural and unwise. To follow this procedure robs the people of their right of expression and desire in this regard. It cannot be considered that deacons thus elected are the choice of the people. They would not feel responsible to the people but only to the pastor who appointed them or secured their election. The Holy Ghost is resident among the people of God, and it is becoming for a pastor to recognize this fact. As Christ shares with His church the privilege of ordination to the ministry (John 5:16; Acts 14:23), so the pastor should share with his people the privilege of the choice of deacons. If he usurps this prerogative to please himself, it is an indication of his tendency toward the autocracy which is forbidden to the ministry. It robs him of the balance which he needs in the operation of the church and the tie into the body of the church as servant and brother beloved.

Notice the specific Scriptural pattern that is given us. "The twelve called the multitude of the disciples unto them and said, . . . Look *ye* out among you seven men." "And the saying pleased the whole multitude, and they chose." Acts 6:3, 5, 6. This scripture tells us that at the instruction of the twelve the multitude of the disciples themselves looked out from among them seven men, chose them by name, and then set them before the apostles. This is a choosing by the people of their own deacons. Of course, the approval and ordination of God also was involved in this matter. The apostles ratified the choice of the people. They considered that they themselves appointed these deacons; they laid hands upon them and prayed. Thus the Lord through the pastors accepted the choice of the people, and the election was complete. If this pattern is followed in the election and installation of deacons in our churches, we can rest assured that it is exactly according to His will and desire.

The function of the deacon board is something of real importance in church life. Sometimes, because of lack of instruction and understanding, deacon boards err in one of two directions: either they are overly impressed with their importance and exceed their prerogatives, or else they do not measure up to the responsibilities which are placed upon them. A careful examination of what the Bible teaches concerning their duties will be all that is necessary in most cases to make them the efficient, helpful co-workers that they are intended to be.

It is clearly to be seen that the purpose which was in mind when they were chosen and appointed in the first place was to take care of the daily ministration—"to serve tables." In other words, it was the material matter of providing the food and physical necessities and making fair distribution of the same. This gives us to understand that to the deacon board should be committed the administration of the material matters of our present-day churches. To serve as trustees of the property is included herein. To see that the building is kept in good repair, to employ and supervise the janitor, and also to feel responsible for the support of the church in all of its departments; these all come within the realm of the deacon's ministry. Inasmuch as the pastor serves as chairman of this board, he should have some interest and voice in these matters. However, he should not carry the chief responsibility regarding them. It would be a splendid contribution toward the pastor's efficiency, and the operation of the church according to the New Testament pattern, if the deacons would take the main responsibility for all the financial and material matters of the church.

Considering the fact that there are high spiritual qualifications required of the deacons, it has come to be an accepted and workable practice that the deacons should serve as an advisory council to the pastor in spiritual matters also. This can be taken as a development which has been ordered by the Holy Spirit and which has His distinct approval. This is to be believed for these reasons: The pastor needs an advisory council, since there is no longer a plurality of elders in a local church. The deacons are the chosen representatives of the people. They are laymen, and are members of the church with the rest of the congregation, and therefore are in a position to know and feel the people's standpoint. Fellow members of the church will confide in them where they hesitate to speak to the pastor himself. This will put the deacons in a position to report to the pastor the exact sentiment of the people, and make him better advised concerning this than he could be alone. This will render them of real value and cause him to appreciate them the more.

A word of caution is needed here. Although it is wholesome and profitable that the deacons should advise and counsel with him freely concerning the spiritual welfare of the church, yet they must remember that they are not anointed as the pastor of the people and hence must not intrude into the realm which is exclusively his. Miriam and Aaron, although serving a God-ordained place and ministry, were nevertheless rebuked of God when they considered that they were equal with Moses. Numbers 12:12. Korah was a Levite and thus had a partic ular ministry ordained of God, but when he felt that Moses and Aaron were not better than he and should not lift themselves above the congregation, God was exceedingly angry and destroyed him and his confederates. Numbers 16. The proper Scriptural example is that of Aaron and Hur in Exodus 17:12. These men stood side by side with Moses, being very close to him, and faithfully held up his hands; they supported him in the spiritual work to which he was called. How beautiful it is for deacons to stand loyally and respectfully by their pastor, hold up his hands in all things, and serve fully and efficiently in the place where God has put them.

We can summarize the relation of the deacons to the pastor in the word "co-operation." Included in this word we mean conference and companionship in working, not excluding the features of respect and obedience. In 1 Thess. 5:12, 13a we read, "Know them which labor among you and are over you in the Lord, and admonish you, and esteem them very highly in love for their work's sake." And note the quotation in Psalm 105:15, "Touch not Mine anointed, and do My prophets no harm." It is right and proper in the sight of God that a deacon should maintain a wholesome respect for the anointed ministry of the pastor of the church. This can go as far as the writer of the Hebrews has enjoined, "Obey them that have the rule over you, and submit yourselves." Heb. 13:17.

If it is to be protested that the pastor may get out of the will of the Lord and manifest a spirit that is not Christlike, then there is a scripture to keep in mind. "Who can stretch forth his hand against the Lord's anointed and be guiltless? As the Lord liveth, the Lord shall smite him; or his day shall come to die; or he shall descend into battle, and perish. The Lord forbid that I should stretch forth mine hand against the Lord's anointed." 1 Sam. 26: 9-11. The Lord will surely control the pastor if the recourse of the deacons is to prayer and patience. God will not allow His vineyard to be trampled upon too long. A wrong on the part of the pastor will not justify an equally wrong spirit on the part of the deacons or the people. God is still on the throne and will correct even His anointed when other measures for their guidance and control have failed. The passage in 1 Thessalonians 5 which was quoted above concludes with the words, "and be at peace among yourselves." No deacon is justified in leading a rebellion against his pastor. If the occasion is serious enough, legal appeal may be made to the proper denominational officials.

Our concluding comment regarding the work and place of the deacon is to remind ourselves that God Himself in His Holy Ghost economy has a special gift of the Spirit for those who are to serve in this capacity. In Rom. 12:6, 7 and 1 Peter 4:11 it is stated that "ministry" is a gift of the Spirit. This word comes from the stem "diakon" which also is the base of our word "deacon." To be a deacon, then, is to serve or to minister, and God has provided a special gift for such workers. It is for the church to discover and honor, by election to office, the one whom God has already endowed with this gift. Also they who have been chosen by the people can ask the Lord to equip them with this Holy Ghost gift for the work that is theirs to perform. They are told specifically in 1 Tim. 3:13, "They that have used the office of a deacon well, purchase to themselves a good degree, and great boldness in the faith which is in Christ Jesus." This means that the degree which the Lord will place behind their name in glory will be one of real value and worth. They have done their part to receive from the Lord an enduement of divine boldness in the faith which is in Christ Jesus. How sacred and how blessed, then, is the office of a deacon, and how important and necessary the work which he performs in the church.

# CHAPTER 14

## The Church as a School

THIS conception is not a common one. We are likely to consider the church as a temple more than as a school. The church is a temple, but equally so must it be a place where the truths of God are taught as in a classroom.

Abraham has given us a beautiful Old Testament precedent in commanding his children and household after him. Gen. 18:19. When the children of Israel were invited by Pharaoh to have the men go and worship God, they insisted, "We will go with our young and with our old, with our sons and with our daughters." Ex. 10:9. At the end of the wilderness journey, as they were contemplating permanent residence in the land of Canaan, Moses repeated the commandments of God with this instruction: "And thou shalt teach them diligently to thy children, and shalt talk of them when thou sittest in thine house, and when thou walkest by the way, and when thou liest down, and when thou risest up. And thou shalt bind them for a sign upon thine hand, and they shall be as frontlets between thine eyes. And thou shalt write them upon the posts of thy house, and on thy gates." Deut. 6:7-9. Likewise, in Deut. 11:19, 20 we read: "And ye shall teach them your children, speaking of them when thou sittest in thine house, and when thou walkest by the way, when thou liest down, and when thou risest up. And thou shalt write them upon the doorposts of thine nouse, and upon thy gates." When Ezra was pleading with the children of Israel for separation, there was assembled unto him out of Israel a very great congregation of men and women and children. They all stood together as Ezra pleaded with them to return to full obedience to the divine command. Psalm 78:1-8 is a passage which emphasizes the need of transmitting the message of the elders to the children: "That the generation to come might know them, even the children which should be born; who should rise and declare them to their children." Solomon also has reminded us, in Prov. 22:6, "Train up a child in the way that he should go." Here is the Old Testament foundation for New Testament and present-day practice of including the children in our gospel ministration.

There is scant information concerning the practices of the Jews after their re-establishment in Palestine and thereafter until their dispersion in A.D. 70. What records there are have come through references in extant writings and through tradition which tell us that Jewish children from an early age attended school in the synagogues. They were taught by the rabbis their whole knowledge of literature from the sacred scrolls. Their very ABC's and ability to read and write were based upon the reading of the Old Testament Scriptures. The interlocutory method was used in which the teacher's skill was in provoking thought and discussion by pointed and adept questions. The pupils themselves were entitled to ask questions in return. Thus they were taught to think for themselves as well as to become thoroughly familiar with the Scriptures. It seems that at the age of twelve the children were graduated from a certain type of instruction and were given the privilege of entering into discussion with their elders, even apart from school session, concerning the things of the law. It was at this age that Jesus went into the Temple, "sitting in the midst of the doctors, both hearing them and asking them questions." Luke 2:46. Thus we know that Christ Himself went through the regular rabbinical school in His childhood. Luke 4:16 tells us that it was His custom to go to the synagogue at Nazareth every Sabbath day. In like manner the apostle Paul, having completed local training at his home in Tarsus, went up to Jerusalem to sit at the feet of Gamaliel. Acts 22:3. This is further foundation and precedent on which New Testament and general church practice has been built. It was honored of Jehovah and has contributed strongly toward the preservation of the Jewish nation down to this present day.

The importance of teaching as a part of the ministry of the church is given strong emphasis by the precedent which our great Head and Founder has set in this regard. He was known as Rabbi or Teacher far more than by any other title. Nicodemus said, "Rabbi, we know that thou art a teacher come from God." John 3:2. The so-called "Sermon on the Mount" was in reality a most remarkable example of the teaching of Christ. Matt. 5:1, 2 says: "And seeing the multitudes, He went up into a mountain: and when He was set, His disciples came unto Him. And He opened His mouth, and *taught* them, saying . . ." We are told in Matt. 9:35 that Jesus went about all the cities and villages teaching in their synagogues, and preaching the gospel of the kingdom, and healing every sickness and every disease among the people."

The ministry of teaching stands out also very prominently in the Great Commission for, although Mark records, "Go ye into all the world and *preach* the gospel to every creature" (Mark 16:15), Matthew says, "Go ye therefore and *teach* all nations, baptizing them . . . and *teaching* them to observe whatsoever I have commanded you." Matt. 28:19, 20. The word "teach" occurs twice in Matthew's version of the great commission. By this we can see that it is at least equally the command of our Master that we go and teach the people of the world as to go and preach the gospel to them. As Matthew says, we teach them into the confession of faith in Christ, then baptize them and then continue to teach

[ 191 ]

them thereafter all the things that Christ taught His
first disciples. This is the Great Commission. Do
we dare to neglect and disobey it?

As the early disciples obeyed implicitly the command to tarry to receive the Baptism of the Holy
Spirit, so likewise it is recorded that "daily in the
temple, and in every house, they ceased not to teach
and preach Jesus Christ." Acts 5:42. They obeyed
the Commission implicitly, teaching and preaching
Jesus Christ. All through the ministry of the
apostles as recorded in the Acts of the Apostles down
to its very last verse they were "preaching the kingdom of God, and teaching those things which concern
the Lord Jesus Christ." Acts 28:31. The workers
were *preaching* and *teaching*. If this was the precedent of Christ, the precept of the Great Commission,
and the practice of the early apostles, can we not
take it as an abiding principle that we likewise should
devoutly give as much emphasis to teaching the gospel
as we do to preaching?

In the divine economy of church offices, gifts and
ministries, the ministry of the teacher is firmly fixed
and is of great importance. 1 Cor. 12:28 tells us
that God has set in the church apostles, prophets, and
teachers; after that, other gifts such as miracles,
healings, helps, governments, and tongues. This is
confirmed in Rom. 12:7 and Eph. 4:11. Distinct
gifts of the Spirit are provided which qualify and
equip those whom He has set as teachers in the

Church. Thus it is clear that in the function of the Church the Lord has made the position and work of the teacher very high and important. This is the standard in a Spirit-filled church. To be a divinely anointed teacher is to operate under the anointing with the gift or gifts which God has given.

The ministry of teaching in the New Testament Church is so important and fills so large a place in the operation of that Church that it is impossible that one man should do all the teaching. The Spirit of God is the great Teacher, and all Spirit-baptized people therefore have something of the spirit of teaching within them. It is for the pastor to provide opportunity to as many as will to give expression and exercise to this gift of teaching within them. The various departments of the church which serve especially as teaching agencies are the Sunday School, the Vacation Bible School, and the Weekday Religious Instruction classes. As these departments function fully and efficiently there will be a constant stream of teaching going forth to the various members of the constituency. This will provide spiritual development for the teachers themselves and a most profitable benefit by the impartation of the Word of God to others. It will be the pastor's duty to oversee the curriculum which is used in these various teaching agencies so that there will be no overlapping but a careful correlation between them.

In the matter of the choice of teachers and their assignment to classes, let not the pastor consider

[ 193 ]

that their appointment is all that will be necessary as their preparation. There should be a careful, systematic training of the present teaching staff and those who are candidates for such ministry. A background knowledge of the contents of the Bible is foundational preparation. Something of the doctrines of the Scriptures should be explained and taught to these teachers. A knowledge of the characteristics of the children and young people, at various ages will be of great value to the prospective teacher. He ought also to be conversant with the principles and practice of the art of teaching. The wise pastor will plan for the development of his school and the eventual need for new teachers as the school grows. Substitute teachers are constantly needed in all departments. The teacher training class will provide these and also the permanent teachers for the new classes that will be formed.

As head and example to the teaching staff of his church, the pastor stands as master teacher. He serves as their example every Sunday morning as he breaks the Bread of Life and imparts spiritual food to his people. There is so much to impart in the way of Scriptural knowledge to his listeners that he will do well to devote one of his week-night services strictly to Bible teaching. This must be thoroughly prepared for and well advertised. It will serve as a drawing card to hungry-hearted people who love to study the Bible. He may follow a textbook, mimeographed notes, or an outline of his own carefully prepared in advance. It will not be amiss for the pastor to assemble all the Sunday School teachers once a week and there with them thoroughly go over the lesson of the following Sunday. Thus he himself will teach the Sunday School lesson through his teachers to the entire school. If the pastor is too busy to teach it or considers it wise to change, he might arrange for different ones of his teachers to teach such a class on succeeding weeks. If the Sunday School is departmentalized, there should be the teaching of the lesson by one of each department to all those teachers that are in that department. As the entire church is mobilized and organized for this magnificent week-after-week teaching of the wonderful truths of God's Word, a marvelous work for God will be done which can be measured only in eternity.

There is a passage in Isaiah 28:9-13 which is very illuminating as we consider the when and how of teaching. There are those who delay the instruction and training of their children until they reach the age of accountability, perhaps about five or six years of age. They contend that little children are too young to know what they are doing and therefore should not be corrected and instructed. How foolish and tragic! It is said that the Catholic Church boasts that, if you will give a child to them until he is seven years of age, they will so indoctrinate him that he will always be a Catholic regardless of subsequent influence. They have made good this boast. It behooves us not to delay the important business of teaching children the Word of God. In Isaiah 28:9 we read: "Whom shall He teach knowledge? and whom shall He make to understand doctrine? them that are weaned from the milk, and drawn from the breasts." This is God's statement that just as soon as children are weaned from the breast their teaching and indoctrination should begin. Let parents particularly observe and practice this. From mother's knee let them learn and know the Scripture. Let babies be listed in the cradle roll of the church. Let them be brought to the nursery class as soon as possible. Through the cradle roll class, nursery, and the beginner department, let them be inducted into the regular channels of the teaching ministry of the church.

The *how* of teaching is here clearly and simply defined. "For precept must be upon precept, precept upon precept; line upon line, line upon line; here a little, and there a little." Isa. 28:10. This is to say that tedious, even monotonous repetition of small portions of divine truth should be continued incessantly until the Word has taken root in the heart. Precept upon precept, precept upon precept, four layers deep. Here a little, there a little, here a little, there a little. Thus, by the well known and most effective method of repetition, the Word of God is implanted in the hearts of the little ones and the older ones as well.

It might be considered significant by some that these verses on teaching precede and follow one of the Old Testament prophecies of the Pentecostal visitation of the last days. "For with stammering lips and another tongue will he speak to this people. To whom he said, This is the rest wherewith ye may cause the weary to rest: and this is the refreshing: yet they would not hear." Isa. 28:11,12. Full-gospel people have the right to conclude that to them particularly is directed this advice as to when children should be taught knowledge and how to teach it.

# CHAPTER 15

## *The Church as a Temple*

**F**ROM the beginning of time it has been the desire of God to come down and dwell among men. In the cool of the day He came walking in the garden calling for Adam and for Eve, that He might have communion with them. To Abraham also He appeared, this time at the height of the day, and after mealtime fellowship together revealed His purpose concerning Sodom and Gomorrah. When the children of Israel came out of Egypt and encamped at Mount Sinai, God said to them through Moses, "And let them make Me a sanctuary; that I may dwell among them." He then filled this tabernacle with His glory so that Moses could not enter because of the cloud and the glory. In like manner, when Solomon's temple was completed as a place in which the Lord could dwell among His people, the glory of the Lord so filled the house that the priests could not even enter. On the day of Pentecost one hundred and twenty disciples let their bodies become the temples of the Holy Ghost and the glory of God came down in such effulgent measure that supernatural manifestations accompanied His incoming and their very bodily equilibrium was disturbed. At last when the full story is told and God's divine plan is consummated, a great voice out of heaven will say: "Behold, the tabernacle of God is with men, and He will dwell with them, and they shall be His people, and God Himself shall be with them and be their God." This series of efforts on the part of Almighty God to come down and dwell among men establishes clearly that this is His fixed purpose and desire. If men would only present their bodies as living sacrifices and gather together in His name in genuine sincerity, He would be there in the midst of them and the place would be filled with His glory. This will constitute any church as a temple.

This presence of God deserves and demands to be respected. When Mount Sinai was smoking and God was coming down to talk to Moses (Ex. 19: 18), He demanded that neither person nor beast should so much as touch the mount or else they would be shot through with a dart. No familiarity or irreverence here! He repeatedly warned the children of Israel through Moses that they should reverence His sanctuary. Lev. 19:30; 26:2. Through the Psalmist He declared: "God is greatly to be feared in the assembly of the saints, and to be had in reverence of all them that are about him." Psalm 89:7. Solomon the preacher has expressed it thus: "Keep thy foot when thou goest to the house of

God, and be more ready to hear, than to give the sacrifice of fools: for they consider not that they do evil. Be not rash with thy mouth, and let not thine heart be hasty to utter anything before God: for God is in heaven, and thou upon earth: therefore let thy words be few." Eccl. 5:1, 2. It is God's specific command that strict reverence be observed when we go into His house.

There are extremes in attitude toward reverence which we might do well to note. One of these is to substitute reverence for reality in worship. The other is, by a fear of this extreme, to go to the other extreme of informality to the extent of irreverence. It would appear that many churches have only a form of godliness without the power thereof. That which is left of their religion is the ceremony and ritual. It seems that they consider that pious reverence of church ritual and deep solemnity in such observance are all that God expects in the way of religion and righteousness. How foolish to consider God as One who observes carefully the details of religious ritual and demands a holy awe in church worship on Sunday and then is utterly oblivious of the moral character and the conduct of the worshipers through the week. Such formalism is altogether in vain.

The reaction from this formalism, however, with the glorious reality and spiritual freedom which there is in Holy Ghost worship and the delightful informality of it, may in some cases have been taken to the extreme of disrespect and irreverence in the house of God. This is the point at which informal worshipers need to be careful. Laughing and talking before the service commences, and immediately upon the pronouncement of the benediction, are breaches of that reverence which we owe to the house of God. Whispering during the conduct of the services likewise is not only a breach of reverence but of good manners as well. It constitutes not only disturbance to those seated nearby, preventing them from hearing the service, but is a distinct stumbling block to those who consider that the house of God should be respected and revered. What should be said of allowing little children to play in the back of the church or in the aisles while an altar service is in progress? This is not only the responsibility of the parents of the children but that of the pastor as well. The children belong to the parents but the church is the responsibility of the pastor. He should not allow his church to be made a place of play at any time, particularly when prayer is being offered around the altar. Here is a needless stumbling block placed in the path of those who are seeking the deeper truths of God. Let us be careful to take out these stones as we prepare the way of the people, a highway to God.

It is in literal obedience to Psalm 100:2, "Serve the Lord with gladness: come before His presence with singing," that nearly all religious services begin with singing. The following Scriptures are typical of the Scriptural command to the people of God to lift up their voices in praise unto Him: Psalm 5:23; 67:5; 92:1; 95:1, 2. In Eph. 5:18-21 we have a condensed description of a Spirit-filled life. It is to be noted that the first expression of such a life is "speaking to yourselves in psalms and hymns and spiritual songs, singing and making melody in your heart to the Lord." It is instinctive and involuntary to the child of God whose heart is clean and whose record is clear to lift his voice in worship and praise to Almighty God. It has been true of revivals all through the years that they have been marked by lusty congregational singing. As a church grows lukewarm and apostate, the ministry of singing is taken over by the choir and the congregation largely is silent. God help us to keep the music ringing in the hearts of our people and in the rafters of our churches. If there is no individual in the church fellowship who is qualified to serve as song leader, then the pastor must substitute in that capacity. Let him put his whole heart and soul in the inspiring of his people to wholehearted spiritual singing.

Let it not be inferred from what is said above that it is un-Scriptural to have a choir. Quite to the contrary. 1 Chron. 16:4 tells how David appointed a choir. 1 Chron. 23:30 repeats the record of their appointment. 2 Chron. 5:12-14 calls attention to the fact that the singers were arrayed with white linen. This is not necessarily to advocate a robed choir but to call attention to the fact that such would have Scriptural precedent if there were one. Uniformity, simplicity, and modesty could thus be insured for a choir of ladies. On the other hand, we are eternal enemies to empty formalism and ritualism. If a robed choir would contribute to empty formality and dead ritualism, then it would be a distinct liability in public worship.

As concerning special singing, the most special that is possible to have is that recorded in 1 Cor. 14:15. When Paul here says, "I will sing with the spirit," he is talking about the gifts of the Spirit, principally tongues and their interpretation, and prophecy. Singing with the spirit here would be a distinct supernatural manifestation. How marvelous and Scriptural it would be if such could be heard more often in our services.

Our God is entitled to our very best. Let those that sing special numbers take the appointment as a serious and wonderful opportunity to represent the people in singing the praises of God. A consecrated voice lifted in holy praise brings satisfaction to the heart of God as well as inspiration to those who hear. It can be taken as a definite rule of procedure in a Spirit-filled church that no unsaved or worldly singer should exercise his talent in special singing. If such are in the audience and take part in the congregational singing there could of course be no objection, but to be appointed by the pastor for public ministry in this regard is contrary to the whole tenor of the plan of God. Isa. 52:11 says, "Be ye clean that bear the vessels of the Lord." If God is provoked at sinners who presume to speak His Word (Psalm 50:16, 17), can we not expect Him likewise to be provoked at those who presume to sing His praises?

In 2 Cor. 4:5 Paul declared, "We preach not ourselves but Christ Jesus the Lord." If we are not to preach ourselves (that is, not to display ourselves and our talent in our preaching), neither should this be done in gospel singing. It is not the song that displays the range and tonal quality of the voice that should necessarily be chosen. Let no human talent be displayed for human admiration, but let all singing rather be sincere and humble and only for the glory of the Lord.

It may be an occasion of surprise to most of us to note in 1 Chron. 25:1 that David and the captains of the host separated to the service those who should prophesy with the harp, with psalteries, and with cymbals. The gift of prophesying has always been associated with the speaking of words for the edification, exhortation, and comfort of the people. 1 Cor. 14:3. Tongues plus interpretation are equivalent to prophecy (1 Cor. 14:5), for this is uttering words which through the interpretation will be understood. When the Lord took the spirit of Moses and placed it upon the seventy elders of Israel they did prophesy. The gift of prophecy was quite common in Old

Testament history as well as in the New Testament church. But in all other places it had to do with the speaking of words that could be understood. But here it is plainly said that the playing of instruments to the glory of the Lord could be so inspired that it would be lifted up into the very realm of prophecy itself. How spiritually excellent then can instrumental music become! An orchestra or a band can be dedicated wholly to the service of God and become absolutely holy in such service. How much people miss when they exclude the use of all instrumental music from their worship!

Let instrumental music likewise be to the glory of God and not simply to win praise of men. As numbers are played that are familiar to the listening audience even though no song is sung in accompaniment, the very words which the music suggests can provoke praise and worship in the hearers. It would seem, as with the singing so with the playing, that purely secular music without the spirit of worship and without a message of a spiritual nature is out of place in a service where God alone is to be worshiped. 1 Chron. 16:4-6 and 2 Chron. 5:12-14 are scriptures which speak of musical instruments and singing being used together in the worship of God.

It is said that worship is a lost art. How true this is. Sitting under an awesome fear is not necessarily worship. Respect for the modern house of God is not to be considered worship either. Worship is the vibration of the soul in the presence of God, the reaching out of the deepest emotions to the God who is above. It is personal, real and warm. It is oblivious to those around and does not depend upon concert of action to enable it to function. It is a consciousness of the presence of God and a response to that consciousness, and a love for God which proceeds from the heart as the expression of the deepest soul.

Our Lord told the woman of Samaria that they who worship God must worship Him in spirit and in truth. True worshipers, He said, should worship Him thus. The Father seeketh such to worship Him. In spirit and in truth means from the inner part of man, and in all sincerity and reality. Church services should be the place above all others where Christians are permitted and encouraged to pray out their hearts in worship of God. How hurtful to the Spirit of God, the church of God, and the cause of God that true worship should be quenched, stifled, and crowded out. There is a distinct command, "Quench not the Spirit." 1 Thess. 5:19.

Spirit-filled churches of these last days have done much to recover this lost art. They have become conscious of the truth of the Scripture which says, "Where the Spirit of the Lord is there is liberty." 2 Cor. 3:17. They have been permitted and encouraged by their leaders to give expression to the feeling of their hearts even though that expression

comes forth in audible tones and in physical dem-
onstrations. This should be appreciated and hailed
as a restoration of that which is vital in the work
of the Lord.

It is so easy to develop a ritual, a perfunctory performance of religious ceremony. There is need to
guard jealously this beautiful freedom and spirit of
worship. Ritual can be developed in so called informal churches too. Ritualism is doing the same
thing over and over again in Christian worship
until it becomes meaningless, a mere church habit.
There can be a certain number of songs, standing
as the last is sung, requests for prayer, prayer, announcements, offering, special song and sermon in a
routine way, which becomes just as much a ritual as
those of the older established churches.

We have a treasure committed unto us. Let us
steadfastly refuse to let hurry, the spirit of our times,
stampede us through the various features of our service. Let us stand constant guard against the ritualism that would crystallize around us. We must preserve a beautiful spirit of worship and liberty in the
Holy Ghost in our services. The Holy Ghost must
have full opportunity to settle down in conviction
or in blessing upon the people. The people must
have time in which to rest in the Lord and to open
their hearts in worship to Him. Let us be deliberate.
Let us keep in touch with heaven. The pastor must
let the Lord speak to him and lead him definitely as
he leads the people in genuine worship of the Lord.

The former Methodist practice of the class meeting, in which individuals took part in testimony and exhorting, finds its present-day counterpart in the testimony service. This is a meeting, or a part of the meeting, that is given over to the people, in which each may express in a few words what the Lord has done for him. To do so is quite Scriptural. "Let the redeemed of the Lord say so, whom He hath redeemed out of the hand of the enemy." Psalm 107:2. The Scripture has said, "They overcame him by the blood of the Lamb and by the word of their testimony." Rev. 12:11. Jesus said, "We speak that we do know and testify that we have seen." John 3:11.

The benefits of public testimony are many. They constitute confession with our mouths which, in addition to believing in our hearts, according to Rom. 10:9, 10, leads to salvation. The Lord said to Joshua, "Every place that the sole of your foot shall tread upon, that have I given you, as I said unto Moses." So we, too, by an act of faith and verbal confession of that faith, take possession of that land which is ours. Testimonies provide great encouragement and inspiration to those who hear. They are evidence to the people from some of their own number that the thing the preacher has been talking about is practical and possible in everyday life. If others like unto themselves have actually received this divine blessing and experienced it in their own souls, and find overcoming grace day by day, here is proof positive that it can be done and great encouragement to the hearers to find such reality in their own lives as well.

The assembly of the saints is also a proper place for the exercise of the gifts of the Spirit. To the Thessalonians Paul wrote, "Quench not the Spirit. Despise not prophesyings." 1 Thess. 5:19, 20. To the Corinthians he said, "Covet to prophesy and forbid not to speak with tongues. Let all things be done decently and in order." 1 Cor. 14:39, 40. "Follow after charity, and desire spiritual gifts, but rather that ye may prophesy." The functioning of these gifts in the church today is the will of God as much as it ever was. Their loss to the church is a great loss which God never meant us to suffer. This is the age of grace and the dispensation of the church The church began on the day of Pentecost and was equipped with the marvelous gifts of the Spirit. As long as the church remains in an unbelieving world, so long has God provided that she should be equipped with these marvelous manifestations. Let the pastor see that these gifts exist and are "stirred up" as Paul said to Timothy (2 Tim. 1:6), and that they have their proper exercise.

These gifts of the Spirit are given to every man to profit withal. 1 Cor. 12:7. They should be controlled by the law mentioned in 1 Cor. 14:12. "Even so ye, forasmuch as ye are zealous of spiritual gifts, seek that ye may excel to the edifying of the church." When the church is in session those gifts which operate to the edifying of the church are the ones which should find expression. The gift of prophecy is emphasized as the one rather to be desired than others. 1 Cor. 14:1, 4. Tongues plus interpretation equals prophecy, as declared in 1 Cor. 14:5, but tongues without interpretation in the church is profitless to the people and is as if the speaker were a "barbarian" (foreign in language) to the audience. 1 Cor. 14:19, 11. It is a trick of the devil to push earnest souls over into an unregulated exercise of these gifts. This can properly be called fanaticism. Satan's purpose is to create reaction against all gifts so that the church will be content to remain without their presence and power. But there is no need that there be any excess in the operation of the gifts of the Spirit. A simple, earnest study of 1 Corinthians chapters 12, 13 and 14 and a careful observance of the regulations contained therein will lead to an operation of the gifts which will be beautiful and to the glory of God.

It is the custom in many churches that there be a public reading of the Scripture every Sunday morning. The pastor reads alone or else leads in responsive readings. To the minds of some this is associated with the formality which prevails in many churches. But the reading of the Scripture has not produced this formality. The reading of God's Word with expression, meaning and reverence does produce wholesome spiritual benefit among the people. It was the custom in Israel in olden days to read the law in the presence of all the people. Deut. 31: 11, 12. Jesus Himself, our excellent Example, went into the synagogue and stood up to read. The very passage that He read is told us (Isa. 61:1, 2a). This practice was maintained among the Jews later as is shown in Acts 13:15, 27 and 15:21. A distinct blessing is invoked on those who read Revelation. Rev. 1:3. From these scriptures one is justified in carrying on this age-old precedent of reading the Scriptures in the presence of the people. But let one's soul be in the reading. The clear thought and even the feeling of the passage should be conveyed in the intonation and emphasis of the reader. Let us make the Bible talk as we read it and the people will be greatly blessed thereby.

Receiving the tithes and offerings of the people is an accepted part of Christian worship. One tenth of our income belongs unto God and is not ours to give. It should be brought to Him regularly. Our offerings are such as we care to give from the nine-tenths that is ours to spend after His tenth has been paid. God has specifically instructed us in Mal. 3:10, "Bring ye all the tithes into the storehouse, that there may be meat in Mine house; and prove me now herewith, saith the Lord of hosts, if I will not open you the windows of heaven, and pour you out a blessing, that there shall not be room enough to receive it." It is stated in Prov. 3:9, "Honor the Lord with thy substance, and with the firstfruits of all thine increase." Do not forget that this is distinctly an act of worship. It should be exalted and dignified as such. Let there never be an apology for receiving an offering. If it is to be apologized for then it should not be done. Clothe it with the dignity that the Lord Himself gives it, and let the people enter into it as a part of their true worship. This dignity is not enhanced by telling funny stories at offering-taking time. This may be considered good technique upon a public platform or in a large hall but it is out of place and beneath the dignity of the minister of the gospel when he invites his people to worship the Lord in the ministry of giving.

The last verses of 1 Corinthians 15 have to do with the lofty subject of the resurrection of the dead and continuing faithful in the work of the Lord day by day. The writer proceeds directly (for there was no chapter break in the original manuscripts) to his appeal concerning the collection for the saints. This is no descent from the sublime to the ridiculous, but a continuation in that which is holy and right. Offerings are not an interruption but a continuation of spiritual worship. As the Lord Jesus sat over against the treasury and watched how the people cast in their gifts, so we can rest assured that He today observes not only the amount of our gifts but also the spirit in which they are given. 2 Cor. 9:7.

It is customary in churches that a few moments be given in which to call the attention of the people to the other services of the day or week. These announcements should be pointed, clear, and brief. A fault into which some ministers have fallen is the prolonged exhortation and explanation which accompany these announcements. This is a weariness to the flesh and actually detracts. It has the opposite effect to that which the pastor desires. People will consider that if that is what they have to listen to they will not be so anxious to come to the other services. Mimeographing or printing the weekly bulletin is a means which some pastors have chosen by which announcements can be simplified and expedited. They feel that to put into the hands of every worshiper a written list of the forthcoming meetings is simpler and more effective. Its cost is trivial if the church has its own mimeographing machine.

To many, all features of the service which come before the preaching are called *preliminaries*. While this is something of a reflection on the importance of the earlier features of the meeting, it does serve to emphasize the high importance of the preaching. It is God's eternal decree that by the foolishness of preaching He should save them that believe. 1 Cor. 1:21. This is God's chief method of letting His voice be heard by the people. How extremely important and holy is the moment and opportunity for the proclamation of His Word. For this moment the pastor's whole life has been in preparation. As much as within him is, he should now preach the gospel. He should speak with the authority of

God and with the Spirit of Jesus Christ. In this manner the people will be carried into the very throne-room of God and receive the climax of their having met together; namely, God's own message to their hearts.

At the conclusion of Peter's sermon on the day of Pentecost, the men to whom he spoke asked what they should do. He then instructed them to repent, be baptized, and receive the gift of the Holy Ghost. This seems to be the divine precedent for the practice which prevails among us of seeking decisions following messages given. Particularly is this true of evangelistic services. As Joshua challenged the children of Israel, "Choose ye this day whom ye will serve" (Josh. 24:15), and Elijah on Mount Carmel demanded that the people cease halting between two opinions (1 Kings 18:21), so it is in order for the present-day preacher to challenge his listeners to make a decision for God. While the inquiry room seemed to be the vogue of the previous generation it has now become an accepted procedure to invite seekers to bow at the altar rail. This was formerly called the penitent form, or the mourners' bench. The word "altar" is taken from the Israelitish economy where the burnt altar was the place where sacrifices were offered after the sinner had placed his hand on them, transferring his sin to this substitute. Christ our Passover is sacrificed for us, and we bow at the wooden rail, calling it an altar, and place our hands upon the Divine Substitute (figuratively speaking) that our sins may be transferred to Him. How fitting and simple is this, and how easy to use it as a means for finding God. It also gives opportunity for a public confession of the need of Christ by arising and going forward for prayer. It makes convenient the assistance which earnest Christian souls are so anxious to give to those who are seeking God. As the pastor appeals for responses to his altar call, let him have faith and confidence. This is the climax of the evangelistic service and all Christian hearts and prayers should be focused in sincere expectation that this moment shall yield results to the glory of the Lord.

Whereas the customary use of the altar is as a place where sinners pray through to salvation, yet it is also convenient as a place for tarrying before God for the infilling of the Holy Spirit. There may be those listeners who need healing for their bodies who can come forward to the altar for prayer. A season of public and collective waiting on God in prayer and praise constitutes what is called "an altar service." This is a sacred, holy time and should be fostered and encouraged to yield all possible spiritual results.

# CHAPTER 16

## *Ceremonies*

I T may be a little difficult for
an "informal" preacher of
the gospel to conduct church ceremonies. However,
this is a part of his duty and ministry and he should
familiarize himself with all the ceremonies which a
minister is called upon to perform and learn to
officiate with dignity and precision. The individuals
for whom a church ceremony is performed consider it
a crisis in their lives. They approach it with awe
and reverence. If we do not conduct the ceremony
in the same spirit, it loses the purpose and benefit for
which it was intended. We do not mean that there
should be a stilted, stiff form but a quiet dignified
orderliness which does honor to the occasion. Many
times there are observers who are members of ritual-
istic churches where ceremonies are considered very
sacred. If a minister violates the sacredness of the
occasion it is quite a shock to those observers and
causes them to lose respect for him and his church.
For these reasons all ministers should conduct the

various church ceremonies with dignity and decorum at the same time expecting the presence and blessing of the Lord on such occasions.

The *marriage ceremony* particularly is one which must be observed carefully. It has legal value and should therefore be strictly and carefully followed. Before the ceremony is conducted, it will be necessary for the minister to acquaint himself with the laws of the State in which the wedding is to be performed. Laws vary in the different States, some requiring that the clergyman be an ordained minister and others permitting licentiates to perform this ceremony. Some large cities require that a pastor be registered in their books as a marriage officer so many days before performing the ceremony.

Ministers should be thoroughly acquainted with the rules of their denomination which govern their right to perform wedding ceremonies. Where it is forbidden to them to officiate in the remarriage of divorced persons, it will be necessary to inquire of the candidates for marriage concerning their previous matrimonial experience. He should never take this for granted, even with young people. Likewise if he doubts the statement of those seeking marriage, he will do well to satisfy himself from other sources before proceeding. One cannot afford to jeopardize himself in the standing of his denomination by carelessness in this matter.

Being assured of legal authority and ecclesiastical approval in marrying a couple, he should then examine their license. After the ceremony is concluded, he should carefully fill in the form provided and secure the necessary signatures of witnesses. Then come the entries in the permanent record book which he must keep. Some States require that all marriages performed by a minister be recorded in a specific book which they have prepared which he must secure at a specified place. Let every minister be very careful to conform to every technicality of the law of the State and County in which he resides or in which he officiates.

If the wedding is to be held in the church or in a private home it is good to have one or more rehearsals beforehand. The minister, groom, and best man appear at the altar, the minister facing the front, with the groom and best man at his left before him partially facing the front. The bride then appears and proceeds slowly, to the accompaniment of a wedding march, to meet her groom at the altar. He receives her there at his left side, and they both then face the minister directly. At this point the actual ceremony begins. Every minister will have provided himself with a good ritual book according to his own taste and conviction.

In conducting *funerals* it will be well for the new pastor to familiarize himself with the customs of the community in this connection. There is a wide variety prevailing throughout the United States in the manner of conducting a funeral ceremony. Cities and rural areas likewise vary greatly. It is recommended that a new pastor should not attempt to change the custom of the community where the funeral is being held but should graciously conform to that custom as accurately as possible. These customs will vary as to the time of the day and week when services are to be held, the form and order of the service itself, and whether or not there shall be a service at the grave with the time-honored committal ceremony. A careful check on all of these matters before the ceremony will repay the pastor and enable him not to violate the traditions of his community, thus coming under censure and blame. Full details for the conducting of each funeral should be carefully arranged for with the loved ones beforehand. Accede to their wishes as far as possible. Use what songs or none as they desire, planning the service to be short or long as they wish.

In officiating at the observance of the *Holy Communion*, proceed calmly and reverently. This is a ceremony which is solemn and sacred and, by the presence of the Holy Spirit throughout, should be expected to yield rich spiritual blessing. Let the most spiritual men of the church co-operate with the pastor in this service, preferably visiting ministers, or the deacons. By a clear understanding beforehand with the co-workers, order and system should prevail throughout. After the co-workers are seated with or immediately before the pastor, appropriate Scripture should be read, preferably 1 Cor. 11:23 to 26 or 31; optionally, Matt. 26:17-20, 26-29; or Mark 14: 12-17, 22-25; or Luke 22:7-20. It is often well to explain that the service is "open communion," but warn unregenerates of danger in partaking. After prayer, the minister reads again the portion concerning the bread, and hands the bread to the workers to distribute systematically among the people. Each person retains his individual portion until all are served. Upon return of workers, they are served by the pastor, and the last one served serves the pastor in turn. All in the congregation then partake along with the pastor and his helpers. The wine is served in the same manner except that all cannot partake simultaneously unless there are individual cups. A suitable conclusion of this ceremony (when held at the close of the service) is to sing a hymn and then quote, "And when they had sung an hymn, they went out." Matt. 26:30.

*Water Baptism* is by immersion and will be observed in one's own or a neighbor's church baptistry or in an outdoor pool or stream of water. The minister should by all means satisfy himself that the candidates understand the ceremony through which they will pass, and that they have experienced a change of heart. Preparatory interview or sessions with candidates are in order. This ceremony is properly held as a part of the Sunday evening service as it has to do with confession of Christ. The solemnity and sacredness of the occasion should be impressed upon candidates and congregation alike. At the proper moment, the pastor relinquishes his pulpit to a fellow minister or song leader, and he and the candidates retire to the dressing rooms to prepare for baptism. The pastor first enters the water, and candidates then appear singly, or, if the ceremony is held in a large open space, the whole group may enter the water together. Distinctly each candidate should be asked: "Do you hereby sincerely renounce the world, the flesh, and the devil, and undertake by God's grace to put off the old man and his deeds, surrendering to the death of the cross and to the grave, of which this baptism is a type, every fleshly lust and worldly desire?" Again: "Do you believe that Jesus Christ, as God's only begotten Son, paid full penalty for your sins on the cross of Calvary, and do you hereby confess Him before men as your personal Savior?" "Do you engage before God and men henceforth to walk by His grace in newness of life worthy of that name in which you are now baptized?" The minister shall then say: "Upon this, the public confession of your faith in the Lord Jesus Christ, and of your determination to leave all and follow Him, I baptize you (full name) in the name of the Father, and of the Son, and of the Holy Ghost" (here submerging candidate entirely). "Amen."

In the *reception of members* into the church, the candidates already will have been found to comply with the requirements of the constitution and by-laws of the local church which they are joining. This ceremony is simply the public "extending of the right hand of fellowship" to those who have already been regularly admitted as church members. Candidates are of two classes: (1) those admitted on confession of faith; and (2) those admitted by letter from a sister church. They can be received alike, or distinction can be made between them, as they or the pastor may desire. It is appropriate to receive new members just before a communion service, that they may partake as members. If the official board of the church so desires, the deacons may co-operate with the pastor in this ceremony. The candidates are seated immediately before the minister who, after reading some appropriate Scripture, addresses the congregation somewhat as follows: "Dearly beloved: the Scriptures teach us that the church is the body of which Christ is the Head, the great family which bears the name of Christ, the army which follows Christ as Captain. We are related to each other as members of His body, as brothers and sisters in His great household, as fellow soldiers in His victorious army. Into this holy relationship the persons before us, having been recommended hereto by the official board of this church, come now to be admitted." The candidates and the whole congregation then arise, the minister saying: "We hereby welcome and receive you (calling each by name) into the membership of this local church, and cordially extend to you the right hand of fellowship in Jesus' precious name." The pastor and deacons then shake hands with each candidate.

In the *dedication of children,* let some children's song be sung while the parents bring the child to the altar and the minister meets them there. Appropriate scriptures can then be read, such as Mark 10:13-16; or Matt. 19:13-15, etc. The pastor then addresses the congregation or assembled friends as follows: "Dearly Beloved, the family is a divine institution ordained of God from the beginning of time. Children are a heritage of the Lord committed by Him to their parents for care, protection, and training for His glory. It is meet that all parents recognize this obligation and their responsibility to God in this matter. Jochebed of old trained her own child Moses after having given him to the Lord. Hannah recognized that her child was Jehovah's. The virgin mother Mary also brought the infant Jesus to the temple. The parents of this child likewise recognize the sacredness of their charge and now bring back to the Lord the treasure with which He has entrusted them. In so doing they recognize and hereby publicly acknowledge their responsibility for the nurture and admonition of this child in the ways of righteousness and godliness."

He shall then address the parents as follows: "In the sight of God and in the presence of these witnesses, do you solemnly undertake to bring up this child in the fear and admonition of the Lord?" Further, "Do you promise early to seek to lead him (or her) to accept Jesus Christ as Savior and Lord?" "Do you promise as far as in you lies to set before him (or her) examples of godly and consistent lives?"

Then taking the child in his arms, or laying hands upon its head, the pastor will say: "In the name of the Lord Jesus I dedicate this child, ————, to God and His holy service." He then offers the dedicatory prayer. The congregation may sing another children's hymn in conclusion.

There are certain other ceremonies which more properly are for the consideration of district officials within a denomination rather than for the local pastor. We refer to the dedication of a church, laying of a corner stone, burning of a mortgage, and ordination of ministers. For these and kindred ceremonies, the church officer will secure a church manual of his own or of a kindred denomination and familiarize himself with the proper procedure.

# CHAPTER 17

# *The Minister in His Study*

THE minister's study is his workshop. He is not in a position to function effectively as a preacher unless he has a room which is devoted to his use as a place for prayer and study and sermon preparation. He is entitled to have this room the very best available. It should be light, airy, and as pleasant as possible. It should be kept comfortable and cozy so that it will not detract from his ability to concentrate upon the task before him. As the woman wants a pretty kitchen in which to spend the many hours needed in preparing meals for the family, so the minister needs and should have a pleasant room in which to spend the many hours that are necessary for him to use in preparation of spiritual food for his people.

The question arises as to where this room should be located, whether in the church or in the home. Privacy should be the main consideration here, and also there is the question of propriety. If he is to be visited in his study in the church by a woman alone, or thrown into too frequent and too private contacts with members of the opposite sex, then this constitutes a danger which he should avoid. To have his wife near at hand on these occasions, as he would have in his home, that he might call her in to sit with him in conference with a woman who might call, is very desirable. On the other hand, to have a study in one's home sometimes results in constant interruption by the patter of little feet and the calls of "Daddy" just outside the closed door. The lady of the home likewise might not have the right appreciation of the importance of his privacy and concentration on his work. If one's time is to be squandered and hindrances are to arise to prevent him from uninterrupted prayer and the study which he needs, then he had better make arrangements to have his study in a place where he will not have these difficulties to overcome.

The best time for study is in the morning. There are two reasons for this: (1) this is the time of day in which his mind is freshest, and in which therefore he can concentrate best and learn the most; (2) these are hours in which pastoral visitation would not be acceptable. Each morning the pastor should find his way to his study and apply himself to this delightful occupation.

The pastor is first of all a Christian, and must take heed to his own spiritual welfare and need. His devotional reading therefore should be the first order of business, not with the thought of gathering sermon

material or making background preparation for his
work, but as food for his own soul. Let him read
a portion of the Word each day. It is good to have
a systematic plan of daily reading which will lead
one through the entire Bible at least once each year.
For possibly one hour each morning let there be a
feeding upon God's Word and a pouring out of one's
heart in prayer.

Concerning the *books* which a pastor will need,
there are certain basic ones without which he cannot
do proper work. As the carpenter needs his tools and
the surgeon his instruments, so there are certain
books which are indispensable to the pastor. We refer to an unabridged Bible concordance, a Bible dictionary, a book on Bible manners and customs, and
a good copy of the Authorized Version of the Bible.
Other versions of the Scripture will likewise be
valuable for comparison and reference. There are
versions prepared by individual men which may be
considered as representing personal viewpoints. Those
prepared by revision committees, such as the American
Standard and more recently the Revised Standard
Version, are to be given greater confidence as pre-
senting more accurately the thoughts of the original
writers. A good unabridged dictionary of the English
language is also considered a necessary tool. A book of
synonyms and antonyms will prove of value. It will
be good to have a few commentaries, too. There are
the time honored works of Matthew Henry and

Adam Clarke, as well as "Handfuls on Purpose," "The Pulpit Commentary," "The "Expositors' Bible," and many others.

In addition, the pastor can build his library with books of a wide variety. First of all come books on theology and Bible doctrine. Hodge and Strong are standard authors here. Broadus' "Preparation and Delivery of Sermons" and Pattison's "The Making of the Sermon," are excellent treatises on Homiletics. Good devotional writers are Andrew Murray, F. B. Meyer, and S. D. Gordon. The pastor will want the sermons of Spurgeon, Wesley, and Moody. Biographical, historical, prophetic, and missionary books will also broaden his study and general knowledge. The books which we will not recommend are those with prepared sermon outlines and books of anecdotes and illustrations. A preacher who cannot construct his own sermons and discover illustrations from the Bible and daily life has his first lessons to learn in Christian ministry.

The preacher owes it to himself and his audience to be informed concerning the affairs of his time and the world around him. There is no end to the reading and studying which he could do concerning secular affairs, and it is not recommended that any large portion of time be devoted to these; but in order to be in touch with the affairs of the world with which his listeners are so vitally connected and concerned, it will be well for him to take one or two of the best secular magazines including one which serves as a digest of the most important reading of the day. In addition to secular magazines and papers, the pastor should receive religious magazines from various sources as well as those of his own denomination; the viewpoint of some other denominations may be found very profitable.

When it comes to the lines of study which the pastor should follow, the departments of his library indicated above can provide many kinds of study for him. The branches of pastoral learning recommended in the chapter on "Preparation for the Ministry" can be followed and explored all through his ministry. As a matter of fact, there will never be an exhausting of the fountain of knowledge and truth. Let him refresh and renew his own mind and replenish his knowledge continually in order that he may have new material to provide for his people week after week.

A word may be in order concerning keeping the various nuggets which he discovers in his reading. There will always be certain points that appeal particularly as he reads various authors. He will find passages that he will consider excellent material for future use. How will he remember where this special material may be found? A filing system can be set up where a record will be kept of this material which he considers of value. Clippings and whole articles from current magazines and papers can be preserved and kept in pockets or envelopes or sections of a filing cabinet marked according to various classifications of Scriptural truth. A card file can be made showing where certain material may be found in the various books which are in one's library. This is an aid to the memory and, even though not used very much, its construction will impress upon one's mind where to find the passages which have been of particular blessing.

What shall be said concerning *sermon preparation?* It is true that this subject is more properly considered in the homiletical field, but Homiletics itself is a subdivision of the general subject of Pastoral Theology. In lieu of a detailed study of the subject of Homiletics, we here offer a few general observations concerning sermon preparation.

The first thing is the text or the theme. What should we preach about? Inasmuch as we are messengers of the Lord of Hosts, it seems only proper that we should go to the Lord earnestly in prayer first of all. What will be His will for us concerning the service that is ahead? Possibly He may have already spoken to our hearts and impressed upon us that message which He wishes us to deliver. Some time previously in our reading, or during our personal visitation work, or in dealing with individuals concerning their spiritual welfare, there may have been impressed upon our hearts a certain scripture or truth as the will of the Lord for us in a future message. He has specifically stated, "The meek will He guide in judgment, and the meek will He teach His way"

(Psalm 25:9), and we may confidently expect His leading in the decision which we must make. "My sheep know My voice." We can hear from heaven and be led definitely by the Spirit in our choice of the sermon subject.

With this matter settled, we proceed to look through the Word of God for His teaching on this subject. From our own general background of what the Bible teaches, we can quickly accumulate scriptures which bear upon the subject. We can likewise jot down our own convictions on this particular point. Relevant articles, clippings, books and comments can then be read and pertinent material assembled.

With all this information and data on hand, we should proceed to arrange it all in systematic order. The thoughts which have to do with approach to the subject should be arranged first. The declaration of God's Word concerning the matter can then be presented. Cause must precede result, and we should proceed logically from beginning to end in the layout of our material. Proper homiletical procedure should be observed in our introduction, presentation, development of thought, and conclusion. Too great detail should not be provided in our notes, or at least not followed too closely, lest we bog down or become lost in the delivery of the sermon. We must be in prayer constantly as we make this arrangement of our material that the Lord will lead us each step of the way.

[ 231 ]

If we have reduced our outline to a few main features and can have confidence in our memory, then let us memorize the various points of the sermon and dispense with notes altogether. This procedure will have stored our mind and heart with the various thoughts in connection with the sermon but will leave to the inspiration of the moment and the definite leading of the Holy Spirit just that emphasis which the various points should receive. We must also pray that God's blessing will rest upon us in the delivery of the message. The anointing of the Holy Spirit is most vital for success in preaching. This unction comes to those who humbly bow their hearts before the Lord to receive it. With this preparation of mind and heart, we can go to our pulpit with the confidence that the Lord will be with us always, even to the end of the sermon.

# CHAPTER 18

## The Minister in His Pulpit

**M**ATERIAL to be presented in this chapter will be found more properly and more fully in a book on Homiletics. We will here only refer to a few matters concerning pulpit manners, care of the voice, and the general subject matter of a sermon.

The platform of a church and especially the place immediately around the pulpit is considered the most sacred of all places in these holy premises. Not only is it sacred but it is the focal point of interest and attention to the whole audience. As the one who occupies this center of the stage, the pastor should be mindful of all his deportment. We would not wish him to be under too rigid bondage, or to be too solemn in his procedure. But here is that place of all places where he should be dignified and proper in his behavior. As he is seated behind the pulpit let him sit upright without any suggestion of a slouch in his posture. When the time comes for him to arise and stand behind the pulpit, he should approach that sacred desk with deliberation and respect. He should not lean upon it, except possibly at some moment in the delivery of his sermon when emphasis requires that he lean forward. In the delivery of his sermon he should not play nervously with any item near at hand nor be guilty of distinctive mannerisms which will distract the attention of his audience. Playing with a handkerchief, buttoning and unbuttoning a coat, constantly taking out one's watch to look at it, and other harmless yet foolish little maneuvers will detract appreciably from the effectiveness of one's sermon. Neither should the hands be in one's pocket or even folded behind one's back. Let every feature of one's physical deportment be as inconspicuous as possible in order not to attract the people's attention away from the word which is being spoken. As the moment arrives in the delivery of the sermon when special emphasis should be given a certain point, then the hands can be called into play and other parts of the body in an involuntary and vigorous gesture. How utterly foolish to imitate someone in the making of gestures, or to practice and execute them in an artificial manner. They should be spontaneous and sincere and only of the kind that are natural to one. A minister is entitled to distinctiveness in gestures, as well as in voice and in the thoughts that are presented. Natural gestures likewise contribute to the impression of sincerity which should be made upon one's audience.

In reference to the control of one's voice, we shall

first comment concerning the wisdom of beginning one's message in a conversational tone. Make your words loud and clear enough to be heard by all in the audience, but be natural and conversational as far as possible. You must win your listeners first of all, and a friendly, easy approach will go far toward gaining their confidence and commanding their attention. As the moment for emphasis comes and the gesture spontaneously breaks forth, there will most likely be a synchronized heightening of the tone and an increase of its volume. This is perfectly as it should be, and will automatically take care of itself. As the Lord gives us perfect ease in the presence of the people and enables us to lose all fear and strain, we will speak as normally and naturally as we do in ordinary conversation. This is an end fervently to be desired.

Never let there enter into your voice any artificial tone or sing-song effect. Why such should ever be can only be explained by the fact that there is a devil who seeks to ruin the effectiveness of gospel preaching. There is utterly no sense in acquiring or using artificiality in public speaking. It may encourage people to go to sleep and may impress them with the professionalism of our preaching, but this is the last thing we want to do.

In considering the subject matter of a sermon, we would warn first that the preacher should not apologize nor make reference to himself at the beginning of his message. Jesus declared, "He that speaketh of himself seeketh his own glory." John 7:18. You are strongly discounting everything that you will say if you advise the people in advance of your inability or lack of preparation. If it is true, they will find it out soon enough, and if not, then you have given yourself an unnecessary handicap. Beware also of the fill-in habit such as a too frequent "amen" or "hallelujah," or any constantly recurrent word or phrase.

We should, of course, use the very best English of which we are capable, and never allow slang or crude expressions to enter our message. The pulpit is no place for lightness or buffoonery. Stories should be told to illustrate and never merely to entertain. When the shaft of the arrow is heavier than its point, then it interferes with its speeding to the target. If the audience will remember your story or illustration and forget that which it was meant to illustrate, then the story or illustration is entirely too heavy and not in proper proportion. In the delivery of the whole sermon be earnest and natural; and, with sweet simplicity and godly sincerity, press home your points to your hearers. 2 Cor. 1:12. This is the way in which God can use us and in which we can bring glory to Him. We must never use the pulpit as a place for self-display, or to win self-praise, but seek in all conscientiousness and earnestness to bring praise and glory to our Lord and Master.

It remains now to be said that the preacher should stop when he has finished his message. "Stand up, talk up, shut up," was the motto of a famous divine.

How utterly foolish to nullify and negate the effectiveness of a message by needless repetition and aimless wandering on after our burden has lifted. We must instantly relinquish the pulpit after having finished the message God has given us. Step out of the way and let God continue His work of conviction in the hearts of the people. Expect definite results from your preaching, and according to your faith will it be unto you. His Word is powerful; expect it to yield results. Be on hand to gather in the grain and to reap the harvest immediately. By all means maintain a high respect for the power and effectiveness of the preached Word and that respect will be shared by the people.

# CHAPTER 19

## *Pastoral Visitation*

WE come now to a department of pastoral ministry which must be considered as very important. It has been estimated that the entire realm of pastoral responsibility and ministry can be considered as consisting of three parts: preaching, visitation, and all other matters. This ranks visiting as equal to preaching in importance. Without any doubt here is a vast department of pastoral work which will open up for the pastor avenues of success which if neglected will leave those avenues closed and contribute to an ineffectual ministry.

The practice of visiting the members of one's flock is not a recent invention; it is not merely a plan of modern ministers. Its roots go back at least as far as Jeremiah and Ezekiel. Through these prophets of old the Lord sent messages to those individuals whom He had appointed shepherds or pastors of His flock. These individuals had been remiss in their responsibility and the Lord rebuked

[ 238 ]

them sternly. 'Woe be unto the pastors that destroy and scatter the sheep of My pasture! saith the Lord. Therefore thus saith the Lord God of Israel against the pastors that feed My people; Ye have scattered My flock, and driven them away, and have not visited them." Jer. 23:1, 2. Through Ezekiel He said, "Son of man, prophesy against the shepherds of Israel, prophesy, and say unto them, Thus saith the Lord God unto the shepherds; Woe be to the shepherds of Israel that do feed themselves! Should not these shepherds feed the flocks?" "The diseased have ye not strengthened, neither have ye healed that which was sick, neither have ye bound up that which was broken, neither have ye brought again that which was driven away, neither have ye sought that which was lost." "And ye My flock, the flock of My pasture, are men, and I am your God, saith the Lord God." Ezek. 34:2, 4, 31. Thus even of Old Testament leaders of His people the Lord required that they seek after them and visit them.

This principle and practice was observed by the perfect Pastor, the Lord Jesus Himself. It is recorded, in Luke 8:1, that He went throughout every city and village preaching and showing the glad tidings of the kingdom of God. This going throughout every city and village is the picture of a thorough, careful visitation of the various parts of every community, taking care that everyone heard the glad tidings. This precedent was followed by the early disciples as well, for "daily in the temple and in every house they ceased not to teach and preach Jesus

Christ." Acts 5:42. This scripture says "every house" and surely it means that. This reveals that Bible studies were conducted in the homes of the people and every house had its visitor to tell of the Lord Jesus Christ. No wonder the high priest declared, "Ye have filled Jerusalem with your doctrine." Acts 5:28. The apostle Paul followed the very same practice of house-to-house visitation, carrying the gospel to the very firesides of the people. He declared in Acts 20:20, "I kept back nothing that was profitable unto you, but I showed you and taught you publicly and from house to house." Jesus declared that pure religion and undefiled before God and the Father was not only to keep oneself unspotted from the world but also to visit the fatherless and the widows in their affliction. James 1:27. And finally it can be noted that at the Judgment of the Living Nations, as described in Matt. 25:31-46, the individuals who were blessed of the Father were those who ministered in the homes and in the prisons, making personal and helpful contacts with those who were in need.

A pastoral call is a visit to the home of a member of the church or constituency with the purpose of being a spiritual blessing and benefit. This is not a social call or a business call, although in some cases these elements could enter into the visit. But, strictly speaking, it is an exercise of one's duty and privilege as the pastor of a people to bring into their homes that personal solicitation for their spiritual welfare and direct individual ministry to their souls' needs.

Pastoral visitation is a logical manifestation and expression of pastoral love and "the pastor heart." There will be the public profession of concern on the Lord's Day. There will also be the private prayer on behalf of the members of one's flock when alone at home. But this profession and this prayer, if sincere and practical, will impel the pastor to leave the ninety and nine of the public gathering and go after the individual sheep in the home. How can one pray and be seriously concerned about the welfare of another and then not even make inquiry concerning that welfare? How can one ask God to undertake on behalf of the spiritual condition of a certain family without contacting that family personally to see whether or not God has answered prayer, and also to offer oneself as the means in the hands of God for the welfare of that family? Pastoral work must not be a mere profession. It must not be only public ministry and preaching to large numbers. One would thus become intent merely upon preaching theoretical truths and developing oratorical ability and would gradually become cold and professional, detached from the realities of life and the actual heart-and-home conditions and needs of the people.

After all, preaching must be the preparation and presentation of that divine truth which is needed by the people which will be food to their souls. In order to do this intelligently and well it will be necessary personally to know the people to whom one ministers. A handshake at the church door and a passing once-a-week contact will never reveal what is in the heart of a person. There must be the leisurely conversation in which an individual has abundant opportunity to open his heart and reveal the problems of his life. A pastoral call is exactly what is needed in this regard. As the pastor inquires sincerely and tenderly into the spiritual need of the one whom he visits, and asks leading questions to draw out the revelation of that need, he has simply now to sit back and listen and see just what is actually there buried in the heart and hidden behind the usually stolid face. This frank opening of the heart is given to him that he might be a physician of souls and mend or heal the wound or the tear. The Lord will give him wisdom and will flow through him with the tender love of the Good Samaritan, and he will be able to pour in the oil and wine, and tenderly bind up the bruised and broken place. How exalted and divine is such a ministry, and how close to God Himself is the man who can deal thus deftly and effectively with the bleeding hearts of men.

By the very nature of public ministry, only general applications can be made in a sermon; truth is presented in a wholesale fashion. As a matter of fact, it would be unethical and harmful to address public remarks to any individual. But pastoral visitation is not so. Within the privacy and sacredness of one's own home, without an audience of friendly or unfriendly ears, the personal matter can be thoroughly gone into and there is neither embarrassment nor resentment felt. This is the proper place for individual application of divine truth and showing the relation to personal problems of the general teachings of the pulpit. Each individual within the congregation is in need of such an interpretation and deserves individual personal assistance from the man who is the shepherd of his soul. Let not the pastor, however, become dictatorial and legalistic and consider it his right and duty to issue personal instructions to the members of his flock as he visits them in their homes. He should not forbid or command them concerning their personal family matters but only advise them as that advice is solicited and welcomed.

Apart from the Bible and one's own prayer life, there is no better source for sermon material than pastoral visitation. As home after home is visited and a discovery is made of the spiritual state of the people, of the temptations that befall them, and of the subtle attacks of the enemy to which they are submitted, the pastor is now in a position to go to his study and prepare a message which will be most helpful to the people of his congregation. He can now talk about the very thing that they want to hear and need to know. He is within personal reach of them now and is not merely broadcasting in the dark. Such sermons as these really build and lead and help the people. They put fat on their bones, strengthen their spiritual lives, and fulfil the purpose of true gospel preaching.

In contemplating pastoral visitation, the pastor has a number of things to take into consideration. Possibly the first question is, Who needs my visit the most? One's mind will instinctively go first to the sick, and then to the individual who appears to be slipping away from Christian moorings. Then the new converts must have periodic attention and, following that, the regular members of one's congregation. Somewhere in this list also there will be those prospects for Christian experience and church membership of whom he has heard during the past week. Naturally this group will include recent visitors to his church and Sunday School and others who have evidenced interest in his church and ministry. A funeral or a phone call requesting a visit will likewise open the door for him to enter some new and interested home.

It is suggested that the pastor shall keep careful record of the calls he makes. This should not be merely mechanical or with the end of being able to boast about the grand total of calls made within a given period of time, but it should be for the purpose of enabling him to be impartial in visiting and thorough in covering the homes of his constituency. Even unconsciously there might be a decided concentration of attention upon a few and a glaring neglect of others. A faithful recording of visits made and checking over this list to guide one in visits to be made will level out this discrimination and will enable the pastor to be equally true and faithful to all his members. The record also will serve as a rebuke to the pastor for his neglect in the matter of visiting his people so seldom. It will also be a protection against false and sweeping charges that are sometimes made that he visits poorly or with partiality.

Upon entry into a home for pastoral visitation, after the customary greeting, the pastor should begin to direct the conversation into spiritual channels. Let him solicitously inquire concerning the welfare both physical and spiritual of every member of the family. As the story of the need is told, let him be very patient and sympathetic. Develop the art of attentive, sympathetic listening. By no means monopolize the conversation, or project your own personal affairs into what is being discussed. You are there to help the other person in his troubles and not to air or share your own. Await the complete unburdening of the needy heart; then swiftly and lovingly bring the Word of God to bear upon the situation, and give the answer to the question and the solution to the problem which is needed. The visit can be concluded with a reading of Scripture and a time of prayer together. This is not absolutely obligatory and in occasional instances it can be omitted. If guests call toward the close of the visit, or something unusual by way of interruption occurs, then the pastor can gracefully retire and consider that his work has been done.

There can be no definite limit for the time of a pastoral call. If no unusual need exists, ten or fifteen minutes will suffice. But if an urgent problem develops, then take as much time as is necessary to solve that problem. You are not visiting merely to do your duty or to develop a reputation as a pastor who visits. You are there to do business for God and should see that that business is done and done well.

There are a few cautions which one should observe in the matter of pastoral visitation. Some have been intimated above but a summary here may not be out of order. Watch that your calling is not concentrated upon a certain few with whom you are most congenial. Let not your visits degenerate into mere social contacts for your own personal enjoyment. Never become too intimate with members of your congregation, lest later they turn again and rend you and take advantage of the confidences which you have unwisely placed in them. Be careful about indiscreet associations with members of the opposite sex. Never be a retailer of gossip and never betray a confidence which has been placed in you by a member of your congregation. The taking of news from one house to another is a carnality which disturbs even when done by a member of the church; how much more serious is the offense if committed by the pastor himself! It could also possibly be true that some men will develop such a love for pastoral visitation that they will be busy thus to the neglect of their private study and prayer life at home.

With these checks and balances carefully in mind, let the man of God attend carefully to the divine commission which is his to carry the gospel of the kingdom from house to house and from home to home.

# CHAPTER 20

# *Ministerial Ethics*

MINISTERIAL ethics has been defined as "refined morality." It is a high standard of human conduct which involves a courteous consideration of others. The divine injunction is that we should "have compassion one of another, love as brethren, be pitiful, be courteous." 1 Peter 3:8. David of old gave his personal testimony in Psalm 18:35, "Thy gentleness hath made me great." This was the quality that he considered responsible for his greatness. This was likewise a characteristic of our Lord Himself. It is also listed as one of the fruits of the Spirit.

In considering this theme, let us classify our comments under relationship to predecessor, successor, evangelists, visiting ministers, and other pastors, adding some general observations.

It can be stated simply, with relation to one's predecessor, that one should honor him sincerely.

Whether he has been extremely popular and has left of his own accord, or has had the misfortune of being unpopular and was removed from office, it still remains for his successor to extend to him honor and consideration. Remember he has been and is your brother in the faith. A reflection upon him is a reflection upon yourself and the church body of which you together are members. Surely he did *some* good in the pastorate which he held before you, and possibly did *much* good. This deserves appreciation and commendation. Even if evidence indicates that he was seriously at fault, remember that God alone is his Judge. · "Who art thou that judgest another man's servant?" Rom. 14:4. Then for one's own advantage it will be good to remember that no matter how much of a failure he may have been, there will be some in the audience (his own converts, particularly) who will love him dearly and resent any reflection which is made upon him. It will behoove the pastor, under all circumstances, to speak well of his predecessor and express appreciation of the work which he has done. His references should be truthful and not extravagant, or else it will be revealed that they are not sincere.

It will also be the part of wisdom for a new pastor not to change the methods of his predecessor immediately. This would constitute a practical disrespect to the previous pastor which will be quickly observed by his friends. Also remember that the other man had longer experience with that local situation than you have had as yet, and might have had reasons for his plans of which you are not now aware, and which, if you knew them, would lead you to do the same. Also it could be that others in the church had to do with the forming of those plans and the following of those methods, and hence your drastic alterations would be an offense to them as well as a reflection upon your predecessor. You really need time to get acquainted with the various phases of the local situation before coming to conclusions as to the best method and policy to be followed. We do not mean to imply that you should always adhere to the methods that you find in vogue, or that you are not entitled to your own thinking and plan. No David should wear Saul's armor, and no pastor can be expected to be an exact duplicate of another. When you will have learned the local situation and have won the confidence of your people, then it will be time to introduce the changes which your good judgment and your own taste dictate.

There will be personal opportunity to honor your predecessor when he returns to the city on a visit. If you hear of his presence within your town, contact him and call on him if at all possible. This is a courtesy which you owe him, and not the reverse, as is generally considered. If he attends the church service, then recognize and honor him properly. This is courtesy as well as good judgment and anything less would be improper. By all means trust him and reject all suspicion either which originates in your own mind or which is brought to you by honest or malicious informers. Give him the benefit of every doubt and believe no ill concerning him unless it is proved irrefutably.

The time will come when you yourself will be some man's predecessor and will in turn, need to be courteous to him as your successor. If you remain in the pastorate long enough to know whom they have chosen as your follower, be sure to present to the people every good phase and feature of his life and ministry. He needs and deserves every assistance which you can give him to enable him to take effective hold of the reins which you have laid down. For your church's sake, in whose welfare is your own reputation as well as interest, enable the new man to have as complete a welcome as is possible for one to receive. If a reception is held in his honor and you happen to be still in the city, by no means attend that reception. As John the Baptist expressed it, he must increase and you must decrease. Retire gracefully and allow yourself to be eclipsed immediately by the new man who comes on the scene. You would be a big fly in the ointment, and a source of constant embarrassment to your people and to the new man, if you attended his reception.

When you withdraw from a pastorate, by all means sever all relations with it. "When therefore the Lord knew how the Pharisees had heard that Jesus made and baptized more disciples than John, he left Judea and departed again into Galilee." John 4:13. If your new occupation and your financial situation will allow, move away from the city in which your former church is located. This will eliminate many temptations to you and your former people and be of great assistance to your successor. If his people come to you for counsel and advice, this will constitute your opportunity to be loyal and helpful to the man who has followed you. With courtesy and grace listen to their story, but then gently and firmly avoid giving the counsel that they ask for and direct their confidence toward the man who is now their pastor. Explain that you are not now in a position to advise them wisely but that you know their pastor is well able to give them the counsel which they need. Untwine the tendrils of their affections and love gently from around your heart, and place them firmly upon the man who has succeeded you. Your correspondence likewise with the members of the former church should be limited sharply. Without being absolutely rude, it will be best if all such correspondence should cease. At the most, let it be brief and merely social, with a distinct retiring from their close affections as soon as possible. Refuse to counsel them. Let them be weaned away from you entirely as soon as you can. Neither will you ask any member of your former congregation for an invitation to perform any ceremonies in your former pastorate. Again we say, you have finished with the former assembly and the more quickly and completely your relations with them are terminated the better it will be.

Your heart's attitude toward the man who has succeeded you should be one of distinct goodwill. Remember that his success will be to your credit as well. You have loved the people whom he now pastors, and as you sincerely desire their welfare you will be grateful and glad when you hear of his success. A soul is pitifully small and carnal that is jealous of another man's success. That another could do what you have done and even improve upon it should not be distasteful to you. If your conceit requires that the work which you have pastored should suffer when you leave it, then, brother, it is good that you have gone, for you constitute a very questionable asset to the kingdom of God. A man is a poor builder whose work must have his own personal presence in order to sustain it. We should not build Christ's church upon ourselves but upon Him. People should be taught to look at Christ and believe His eternal Word rather than merely to love the man who stands at their head. As you have any opportunity, and on every occasion, direct the love, confidence, and support of your former people to the man who has succeeded you in the pastorate. This is the sensible, manly, and spiritual thing to do.

When you return to the city in which you were

formerly a pastor, pay your respects to the man who succeeded you. Be sure to give no opportunity to Satan or any of his agents to introduce friction between you and your successor. Put him in a position to rebuke all dark hints that you have returned to do him damage. Your personal contact with him as soon as possible will serve to this end. By all means refuse the payment of tithes by his people to you. Such belong to their present pastor, and a man is guilty of stealing who receives that which does not belong to him. Even gifts that are beyond tithing should be weighed carefully as to the propriety of their acceptance. Give God and your successor the benefit of the doubt by conferring with him about all such matters. His friendship and confidence in you are worth far more than the monetary value of the gift that is offered you. If you should be called, without your requesting it, to officiate at a funeral in his parish, then consult with him and give him the place in that ceremony which is acceptable to him and to the bereaved family.

The relation between pastors and evangelists is likewise one which requires a definite code of ethics. It is the devil's glory and the church's hurt when friction and misunderstanding arise between the branches of gospel ministry and between fellow-ministers. The pastor should be most considerate of the evangelist whom he calls to serve him in his church.

If you have a fixed appointment with him, by no means should you cancel that appointment abruptly and close to the time of the scheduled meeting. This is a sacred obligation which you have entered into and breaking it will cause loss to the evangelist. If it becomes desirable to change your plans for the proposed meeting, take the matter up with the evangelist and see whether or not some adjustment can be made that will be satisfactory to you both.

When a man comes to you to conduct a revival in your church, give him free rein as to the conduct of the service and the type of sermon that he is to preach. If you cannot do this, then do not call him in the first place. If you insist upon his preaching your type of sermon, then why call him since your people already have that type continually? Your call to him presupposes your need of a change of ministry for your people. Expect him therefore to be himself and to preach the gospel in his own way from his heart. It will pay you to provide him with every possible comfort, for this will reflect in the peace and attitude of his mind as well as the comfort and strength of his body. A little additional money spent for the physical convenience of your evangelist will more than repay you in the added ability and skill which he will have as a result.

As regards his remuneration, he should be paid as well as the pastor of the church in which he conducts the revival campaign. This stands to reason, for he is occupying the same pulpit. This is the minimum. His traveling expenses to your city and his entertainment while there should be paid in addition. Remember that he doubtless has a home to support and his being away from home necessitates additional expense. There are periods of time likewise in which he must be idle on account of holiday seasons, going from one campaign to another, last-minute cancelations, etc., which cut down considerably his annual income. This requires that your gifts to him shall be generous. Be sure likewise to give him the full amount of every offering that is given for him. No amount of juggling of justice or expediency will justify a pastor in withholding any portion of a public offering which is clearly understood to be wholly for the evangelist. If it is too much in your opinion, then simply learn a lesson not to receive such an offering again. But this offering is his and common honesty demands that you turn it over to him.

In the conduct of the campaign it will be wise to consult with your evangelist frequently and also to co-operate with him fully. A spirit of intimate friendship and cordial fellowship should prevail between you and will result in far greater accomplishment in your revival campaign. Needless to say, the evangelist has many opportunities in which to stimulate the loyalty and devotion of the people to the pastor, and so sheer selfishness alone should cause you to maintain his friendship.

These are rules which work both ways. The evangelist should be just as true and considerate of the pastor as the pastor is of him. He too should not cancel a coming revival, for the pastor has depended upon his coming and it may now be too late to secure another. Advance advertising may also be out and this would mean confusion and hurting public confidence in the pastor and his church. If possible, notify the pastor of the exact time of your arrival. As you minister the Word from his pulpit, be careful that you do not knowingly contradict any particular doctrine which the pastor might have. In every denomination, there are variations of personal opinions about some matters concerning which there is no denominational pronouncement. The matter certainly could not be serious enough to require that you preach it in order to be conscience-clear; and yet it could be serious enough to embarrass the pastor and to require him to contradict you after the campaign is over, and to spend much time undoing the supposed damage which you have done. It is far better therefore to steer clear of all mooted questions and emphasize the great cardinal truths upon which there is perfect agreement. The evangelist should never cast reflection either publicly or privately upon the pastor whose guest he is. If certain disgruntled members take him to one side and begin a recitation of the pastor's faults, or lay the groundwork for an invitation to the evangelist to be their pastor (either of the entire church or a portion of it), then it is his bounden duty to seal off such an approach and definitely to reject all such suggestions.

In the matter of money, likewise, the evangelist should be true to the pastor. He should not receive money from the people without reporting the same to the pastor, so that it can be recorded as a part of the church's gift to him. By no means should the evangelist seek to secure a list of the members of the church either from love offering envelopes or otherwise in order that he might send back periodical letters or copies of his magazine. Any activity whatever which is carried on among the members of the church without the knowledge and approval of the pastor is, upon the very surface of it, unethical and condemned.

The evangelist should seek the counsel of the pastor in the conduct of a revival campaign and should endeavor to co-operate with him fully. It might be better, however, for him to remain un-advised concerning certain particular situations in order that he might be the more free in his preaching. When the campaign is over and the evangelist has left the city, he should refuse all invitations or temptations to return to the same city and conduct a meeting which would capitalize on the previous campaign to the loss of the pastor whom he had served before.

Then there is a question of the relation of the pastor to visiting ministers that may be in his con-

gregation. Of course, he should recognize them
publicly and extend to them the customary courtesy
to be with him on the platform, or to lead in prayer.
It is not advised that he must ask them to preach
if it happens that they appear in his audience quite
often, or if they are members of his congregation
and are unoccupied as ministers at that time. On the
other hand, he should ask them to preach if they
are either his predecessors in the pastorate or senior
church officers, or if it seems otherwise profitable.
Their duty to the pastor if they are a member
of his congregation is to pay their tithes there (if
they are engaged in secular work at the time). They
should certainly not head any faction or be dissident
to the pastor or appear to lead a rebellion in any
wise whatever. They must be loyal to the pastor in
every way, even stifling any convictions of their own
as to how he should conduct his church. They
must remember that this is his church and not
theirs, and every man has a right to pastor his
church in the way he thinks is best. If they are
members of another man's congregation they should
be merely members, and loyal ones at that, and forget
that they are ministers and have a pastor's viewpoint.
They should never criticize him to his members nor
listen kindly to criticism that is poured into their
ears. If a visiting minister has been asked to preach
for a certain length of time, or upon a certain subject, and he accepts this invitation, he should not
preach longer than for the appointed time, neither

should he change an assigned subject without the permission of the one who invited him to speak.

An important field of ministerial ethics is the relation of a pastor to his fellow pastors in the same city or community. The first thought in this regard is that he should not proselyte. As the stealing of sheep in the frontier days was a crime punishable by death, so it remains most reprehensible among ministers that one should induce another's sheep to exchange pastures. If members of another man's congregation attend your church, that is their privilege. However, you are not to visit those members unless they invite you to do so. Even then, it is merely to respond to their invitation to answer whatever questions they may have to ask you. Never should you solicit or intimate that their membership be transferred to your church. This is strictly their own business and something between them and God.

When you are invited to minister at any inter-denominational meeting, be sure never to take denominational advantage of the occasion. Churches sometimes co-operate in a Good Friday three-hour service, Easter sunrise service, Thanksgiving service, etc. If you are asked to speak at such a union, choose that subject which will be acceptable to all of your hearers. This is easy to do within a fundamental fellowship. It is not suggested that fundamentals of the faith ever should be compromised.

Baccalaureate and other public school sermons are in this same class. When preaching funerals of those who do not belong to your congregation, do not present controversial doctrines or take advantage of the presence of those who did not come to hear you preach but came out of respect for the person whose funeral you are conducting. It might be said here also that it is not good taste to preach too long at a funeral, for it is a time of pain to those who are bereaved, and your words of comfort and your message of consolation should be only long enough to make clear to them the blessed hope of the Church and the great abiding presence of the Holy Comforter Himself. Neither should one become too personal in conducting such a service.

In public ministry (over the radio, for instance, or even in one's own church) one should seek to be constructive and charitable rather than to indulge in tirades and attacks upon members or preachers of another faith. It is true that the Lord has instructed us to put the brethren in mind concerning the false doctrines of the last day, and has said that in so doing we should be good ministers of the gospel of our Lord Jesus Christ. 1 Tim. 4:6. We should be faithful to our own people in warning them against apostasy and all false doctrines that may arise. But "knocking" other churches and bitter condemnation of others does not savor of the Christ who loved sinners while hating sin. After all, God Himself is the Judge, and we must not be hasty in passing judgment upon those who call themselves Christians. Such attacks are unethical according to the standards of radio broadcasting companies, and hence must be considered the same when practiced in our own churches.

There are a few general remarks in this connection which can be made concerning miscellaneous matters. For instance, do not give your church roll or a list of the names of your members to any agent or salesman who wishes to solicit them. Neither should one send a beggar or an agent to another preacher or church just to get rid of him. Do not take advantage of your position as pastor of the church to sell insurance or goods of any kind to your members or others.

In your visitation work or in any private relationship with your members, be sure never to betray a confidence which is placed in you. If the doctor or a family should confide in you concerning the danger of a patient, do not violate their wishes in telling that patient of his danger. If a person has made a gift to your church and wishes to remain anonymous, by all means do not disclose the identity of such person. If your church has extended charity to someone, then do not embarrass such an one by public or private statement concerning the gift.

When leaving a parsonage be sure that it is in no worse condition and repair than when you received it. Your official board likewise will appreciate your advising them of any plans which you may have to sublet part of the home to supplement your income.

Do not practice fake advertising; never represent that you will do a certain thing and then fail actually to perform it. People may laugh at your clever deception one time but it will be a case of "Wolf, wolf!" thereafter.

Do not be guilty of plagiarism. It is a sin. To quote another person without giving him credit is stealing his words and taking honor which is not yours. "I am against the prophets, saith the Lord, that steal My words every one from his neighbor." Jer. 23:30.

Do not continue preaching on the same text after your evangelist or a guest speaker has done so. This implies his imperfect handling of the subject and is a reflection on the main speaker. Neither, if you are leading a song service, should you speak at length between the verses of a song if another is the preacher.

Do not pray for your personal needs in public. Such "loud faith" shows neither faith nor good taste. One should not pray for distinguished persons in the audience or be personal in any way.

Do not criticize your own brethren or your church in public. You should never be untrue to the doctrine and standard of your church. If you can no longer concur therein, the ethical thing is to resign.

Do not conflict deliberately with the program of

a neighboring church. If you have been invited by some group leader in another church to speak at a meeting of his group, be sure that you have received the approval of the pastor of that church before responding to such an invitation. One should never receive advances from a church whose pastor has not yet resigned, or ever make advances to such a church.

## CHAPTER 21

# *Paul as a Pattern*

$S$O very important is the work
of the minister of the gospel
that the Lord not only has given us many direct
instructions and exhortations concerning it, but
has also set at the very beginning of His church
dispensation a certain man who in every phase of
his life was an ideal example and pattern for preachers. Paul himself said that it was the plan of the
Lord Jesus to show forth in him first all longsuffering
as a pattern for them which should hereafter believe
on Him. 1 Tim. 1:16. To Timothy his beloved
son in the gospel he cited himself as an example of
Christian character and ministry. 2 Tim. 3:10, 11.
"But thou hast fully known my doctrine, manner of
life, purpose, faith, long-suffering, charity, patience,
persecutions, afflictions." If we study the character
and ministry of the apostle Paul, we will have God's
idea and ideal of a pastor's character and service
which we will do well to follow.

Considering Paul's preparation for ministry, we

will note a few things briefly. He was thoroughly converted. Acts 9:5. He was baptized with the Holy Spirit. Acts 9:17. He was endowed with gifts of the Spirit. 2 Cor. 12:12; 1 Cor. 14:18; 2 Cor. 11:5, 6. And Paul had other than these climactic experiences and visitations from heaven, for there was the waiting before God that he might be taught of Him the wonderful truths of the gospel. His school was in the Arabian desert, the city of Damascus, and away back in his native town of Tarsus. Three years were spent in the first-named places (Gal. 1:12, 18) and an indefinite time (possibly ten years) back at Tarsus. See Acts 9:30; 11:25, 26; Gal. 2:1. During this long period of quiet, personal tutorage, Paul sat at the feet of Jesus and had a personal revelation of the wonderful truths of God. It is true that this was a once-for-all revelation for the Christian Church and is now written down clearly and finally, preserved for us in his Epistles; but it does not follow that we who have and may read this revelation in plain English are able to comprehend its spiritual significance by our own ability. If Paul received it in the first place as he waited before God, surely it should be possible for us in the same way to understand that which has already been given. The way for us to get such understanding is likewise to wait before God and ponder upon His teachings. Paul was not equipped to preach and teach until he first had this clear revelation. How can we consider that we are equipped to preach and teach until we have a clear understanding of that revelation? With all of the glory and special privileges which was Paul's in receiving the revelation of the mystery which theretofore had been hidden from men, he was at the same time willing to be taught and assisted by those who were older in the Lord. Acts 9:27; 11:25-30; 13:2. What a beautiful example he is in all of this.

A far more extensive study is that of Paul's character. His being in contact with heaven to receive a revelation of the gospel in the first place was continued on through his ministry step after step and year after year. Acts 16:6, 7; 18:9; 23:11; and 27:23. Is it necessary to add that he was thoroughly consecrated to his task? From the moment when he asked, "What wilt Thou have me to do?" until he declared on his way to Jerusalem that he was ready not only to be bound but to die also for the name of the Lord Jesus, his life was continually on the altar of God. Acts 9:6; 13:2, 14; 21:13. He was bold and fearless (Acts 19:30; Gal. 2:11) and yet, withal, a tender, considerate, Christian gentleman. 1 Thess. 2:7; Philemon 9. Here is a man that exemplified practically all of the Christian virtues. We will simply cite further his great unselfishness. Acts 20:33, 34; Rom. 9:3; 2 Cor. 12:14.

The amazing knowledge of this apostle has been a matter of wonderment and inexhaustible study for the many generations of students and scholars which have followed him in Christian ministry. His knowledge of the future and the events of prophecy was a supernatural revelation. First and Second Thessalonians particularly, as well as First Corinthians 15, First Timothy 4, and Second Timothy 3, tell us about conditions which will exist at the end of the age, about the catching away of God's saints, the revelation of the man of sin, and the glorious appearing of our Lord and Savior Jesus Christ. Paul's knowledge of the gifts of the Spirit and the administrative organization of the Church, the body of Christ, is revealed and clearly set forth in Romans 12, First Corinthians 12, and Ephesians 4. Such knowledge is of tremendous value, not only to him but to us who study his words and follow his example. The beautiful yet profound mysteries of the gospel seemed not to be mysteries to him but were clearly understood. 1 Cor. 4:1. The mystery concerning the Gentiles, concerning the mystical body of Christ, the mystery of godliness, the mystery of iniquity, and the mystery of the rapture of the Church, were his to know and to "make all men see." Eph. 3:9. The great cardinal doctrines of salvation, the amazing love and exquisite justice of the mighty accomplishment on the Cross, the legal aspects of the atonement as well as its manifold features and extensive triumphs, were all so clear to Paul. (See the Book of Romans, particularly.) He even saw and heard things which were unlawful to utter (2 Cor. 12:4), being evidently more wonderful and more profound than anything which he committed to writing and which is given for our understanding. This phase of the Pauline pattern (his great knowledge) is sufficient in itself not only to give us cause for admiration but to give us occupation and earnest striving in our life and service as ministers of the gospel.

It could easily be that the part of the life of the apostle Paul which was the secret of his amazing spirituality, power, knowledge, and success in gospel work was his suffering for Christ. Here was a man who not only counted all things loss but suffered the loss of all things. Phil. 3:7, 8. He hungered, he thirsted, was naked and buffeted, had no certain dwelling place, worked with his own hands, was reviled, persecuted, defamed, and made as the filth of the world and the offscouring of all things. 1 Cor. 4:11-13. He seemed to glory in these afflictions, for there are many lengthy passages which describe what he suffered for Jesus' sake. Afflictions, infirmities, necessities, persecutions, distresses, reproaches, stripes, imprisonments, tumults, labors, watchings, fastings, stoning, shipwrecks, and perils are set forth in 2 Cor. 6:4-10; 11:23-30; and 12:5-10. These all left marks in his body which he referred to in Gal. 6:17. And to climax it all and to tap a mystery which to many of us seems still unsolved, he declared in Col. 1:24, I "rejoice in my sufferings for you, and fill up that which is behind of the afflictions of Christ in my flesh for His body's sake, which is the church." What cowards we all seem to be in comparison! How we shrink from physical suffering and are not even able to enter voluntarily upon periods of fasting and prayer. Of course, public opinion today is not violently opposed to the preaching of the gospel, and there is small occasion in America for suffering persecution and martyrdom. Could it be that the scripture, "All they that will live godly in Christ Jesus shall suffer persecution" (2 Tim. 3:12), implies and charges that our lives are not godly enough to provoke persecution? Could it be that in our failure to suffer for Christ's sake we have closed for ourselves the door into greater knowledge of the mysteries of the gospel, and greater power and effectiveness in its preaching, and the possession and exercise of the gifts of the Spirit, and the supernatural signs and wonders that accompanied Paul's ministry?

But this is not all about this wonderful man of God. Look now at his prayer life. To the Romans whom he had not visited personally and who it appears were not his direct children in the gospel, he says that God is his witness that without ceasing he made mention of them always in his prayers. Rom. 1:9. His prayer for the believers of the province of Galatia who were about to slip back into the legalism of the law approached the point of intercession and travail as he yearned so intensely that Christ should be formed in them. Gal. 4:19. For the Ephesians likewise he prayed and ceased not to give thanks, mentioning them definitely in his prayers. Eph. 1:16. He says specifically that in every prayer of his he always remembered the disciples at Philippi, making request for them with joy. Phil. 1:4. He prayed likewise for the church at Colosse (Col. 1:9), and for them at Laodicea, and even for as many as had not seen his face in the flesh, having great conflict in prayer for them. Col. 2:1. Neither did he forget the Thessalonians. 1 Thess. 1:2. His son, Timothy, came in for remembrance in his prayers night and day. The climax of this soul-intercession was reached as he brought before God his brethren, his kinsmen according to the flesh. He even offered himself and his soul's eternal destiny as a ransom for the redemption of his fellow Jews. Rom. 9:1-3. We see here that it was not simply preaching, blazing new trails in pioneer Christian work, exercise of miraculous powers or administrative care, and governing the various churches, but it was personal prayer of an intense and incessant nature that had a large part in the character and life of the apostle Paul.

Let us inquire now into the objectives which he had before him in his ministry. Certainly his was not a pointless life, nor was he guilty of aimless wandering and merely doing that which expediency and the chance of the moment dictated. He had specific aims, immediate and long-time goals, toward which he consistently worked and moved. In his own personal life he gives us a glimpse of that which activated him far down the Christian road and even as he approached the end of the race. In Phil. 3:9-14 he sets as his goal that he may win Christ and be found in Him with the righteousness which is of God by faith. He wants to know Him and the power of His resurrection, even more fellowship in His sufferings, and to be made conformable unto His death. He had not reached his goal. He had not yet attained. He was not yet perfect. But he flung away the things of the past, stripped himself for the race, and strained forward—"if by any means I might" win the prize of the high calling of God in Christ Jesus. Oh, how beautiful and how inspiring! How provoking to divine emulation! May God help us all to follow in his train.

In his ministry he had as his objective to make the preaching of the gospel fully known. From Jerusalem on into the hills of Albania he fully preached the gospel of Christ; and in his very last Epistle he rejoiced that he was delivered from Nero's power, and declared that it was "that by him the preaching might be fully known." 2 Tim. 4:17. He strove to make all men see (Eph. 3:9), and he held it as his task and objective to warn every man, to teach every man, and to present every man perfect in Christ Jesus. In this work he labored, striving diligently, and working mightily. Col. 1:28, 29.

For the practical-minded it would be interesting to observe something of the tactics which Paul employed. In his various missionary journeys as he entered new cities and towns, he went to the Jewish synagogue and preached the gospel to the Jewish people first of all. He declared in Romans 1 and 2 that the gospel was for the Jew first, and he practiced this in his own preaching. Acts 13:14, 26; 14:1; 17:2; 18:4-6. Has this policy of gospel preaching changed? Are there not Jews of this generation to whom the gospel likewise should first be preached? Are we faithfully following the Pauline precedent which has been set us? Another of the tactics which Paul employed was to go into areas where the gospel had not yet been preached. Rom. 15:20, 23; and 2 Cor. 10:13, 16. This will not be as easy for us as for him, but we need to be reminded that there are entire countries as well as large portions of others in the world today which do not have a testimony for the Lord Jesus Christ. His commission still reads, "into *all* the world," and "to *every* creature." Paul also labored with his own hands for his personal support and that of those who traveled with him. 1 Thess. 2:9; 2 Thess. 3:8, 9; Acts 18:3. He did not decline offerings from churches already established (2 Cor. 11:9; Phil. 4:16), and so today he would approve of ministers and missionaries in unworked areas being supported by the gifts of Christians.

Finally let us notice that it was the practice of the apostle to explain to his converts every doctrine and phase of the gospel which was committed to him. Acts 20:20, 27; 1 Thess. 3:4; 2 Thess. 2:5. Following this precedent will cause us not to withhold any element of this glorious full gospel that today is entrusted to us. Salvation, divine healing, the Baptism of the Holy Spirit, and the glorious truths of the second coming of Christ, are news which our converts need to be told and truths which will strengthen them in their experience and faith. These are methods which the apostle Paul used and which are still appropriate and effective in the propagation of the gospel.

# CHAPTER 22

## Jesus as Our Example

AS the climax and consummation of all exhortation and precedent which the Bible gives us in the work of the ministry, we have the beautiful and perfect life of Christ. Although very Son of God and unique, "the only begotten of the Father," yet He emptied Himself and was made in the likeness of man, and was in every point tempted like as we are, yet without sin. He placed Himself voluntarily in that position of dependence upon His Father which we are to hold toward Him. With no sins to wash away and no burial of the old man necessary, He nevertheless submitted Himself to the baptism of John, saying, "It becometh us to fulfill all righteousness." We must not reject the example of Christ as one impossible to follow, but rather accept it as the perfect pattern, and obediently follow Him as He has commanded. John 13:15 and 1 Peter 2:21. "As My Father hath sent Me, even so send I you." John 20:21

In His natural birth, Jesus was born of God. This takes place with us at the new birth after we become conscious of our sins and open our heart's door to let Him in. More amazing still, He bowed His head to receive a baptism and anointing of the precious Holy Spirit. This experience came to Him when thirty years of age and as preparation for the mighty public ministry upon which He then launched. Luke 3:21-23; Acts 10:38. The Father gave the Spirit without measure unto Him, and in this divine power He went forth to vanquish the devil in the mount of temptation, to preach the Word in the synagogue at Nazareth, and to launch upon a ministry of mighty words and deeds.

The deliberation shown by Moses and by Paul in the matter of plunging into public ministry was also manifested in the life of Christ. His mother urged Him to perform that first miracle a little before the ordained time. He chided her for this and deliberately awaited the arrival of the exact moment. John 2:4. His unbelieving brothers likewise prodded Him to go up to Jerusalem and display Himself. His reply to them revealed that He was still moving carefully according to His Father's schedule for Him. John 7:3-10. And He knew when the hour arrived for His glorification. John 17:1.

This awaiting His Father's time indicates to us also that He was led very definitely by His Father step by step. He confessed and made no attempt to conceal the fact that He received specific commandments from His Father and was careful to obey them in every detail. John 14:31; 12:49. These instructions from His Father constituted the light in which He walked, and seeing which He could not stumble. John 11:9, 10.

This leads us to the further observation that Christ lived moment by moment in vital communion with His Father. "Verily, verily, I say unto you, The Son can do nothing of Himself but what He seeth the Father do: for what things soever He doeth these also doeth the Son likewise, for the Father loveth the Son and showeth Him all things that Himself doeth." John 5:19, 20. Again He declared, "I can of Mine own self do nothing. As I hear I judge." John 5:30. A double revelation comes to us in this wonderful declaration of John 6:57. "As the living Father hath sent Me and I live by the Father, so He that eateth Me even He shall live by Me." Christ made Himself dependent for very life and breath upon His Father. He lived by means of that relationship, and also declared that we shall live and breathe by Him alone and continue our existence as Christians in this manner.

In His relation to the world around Him Christ did not hesitate to witness concerning the wickedness, and even to pull off the mask of hypocrisy that existed too often around Him. He declared, "The world hateth Me because I testify of it, that the works thereof are evil." John 7:7. To the unregenerate who surrounded Him, He declared, "Ye are of your father, the devil." John 8:44. And to the hypocritical Pharisees He said, "Ye serpents, ye generation of vipers, how can ye escape the damnation of hell?" Matt. 23:33. This forthrightness and discerning candor and faithful rebuke on the part of Christ incurred for Him the wrath of those whom He denounced. This did not deter Him nor cause Him to change His method. He accepted it as the inevitable and as a necessary part of the life and experience which were His. He also faithfully warned and set it as a positive pattern for succeeding generations of His followers that the world would hate them as it hated Him. On the way up Calvary's hill He declared, in beautiful Oriental imagery, "If they do these things in a green tree, what shall be done in the dry?" Luke 23:31. Again, to His disciples, He said, "It is enough for the disciple that He be as his Master, and the servant as his Lord. If they have called the Master of the house Beelzebub, how much more shall they call them of His household?" "If they have persecuted Me, they will also persecute you; if they have kept My saying, they will keep yours also." Matt. 10:25; John 15:20.

In the midst of all the struggle and intense opposition that bore heavily upon Him, and His exposure of the wickedness of His foes, His spirit was always tender and sweet. The great dominant characteristic of His life was that stream of love and infinite compassion that flowed continually from His great heart. "Seeing the multitudes, He had compassion on them." "Having loved His own which

were in the world, He loved them unto the end."
John 13:1. He declared that He the Good Shepherd
would give His very life for the sheep. John 10:11.
Toward His enemies, too, He manifested that divine
forgiveness which has amazed the world ever since.
"Father, forgive them, for they know not what they
do." Luke 23:34. This stream of divine love came
from the very throne of God. "God was in Christ,
reconciling the world unto Himself." And it was
not meant to proceed from Christ alone. "He that
believeth on Me, out of his inmost parts shall flow
rivers of living water." John 7:38. "I in them,
and Thou in Me, . . . that the world may know that
Thou hast sent Me, and hast loved them, as Thou
hast loved Me." John 17:23.

# Index